Our Knowledge of Facts and Values

Our Knowledge of Fact and Value

Our Knowledge of Fact and Value

BY

EVERETT W. HALL

Introduction by

E. M. ADAMS
Professor of Philosophy, University of North Carolina

Chapel Hill

THE UNIVERSITY OF NORTH CAROLINA PRESS

To
Richard John Hall

Contents

Contents

Introduction

WE HAVE before us the last work of Everett W. Hall. It is based on a series of lectures he delivered at Kyoto University, Japan, in 1958-59. He had just completed the final revision of the manuscript at the time of his death.[1] We are very fortunate that he was able to finish it, for it is not only a significant, pioneering work in its own right, but is indeed the keystone to his whole philosophical position. Without it, his earlier books,[2] especially *What Is Value?*, would be incomplete and less convincing. Although *Our Knowledge of Fact and Value* can be read and appreciated by itself, it is part of a larger whole and should be thought of as such. The purpose of these remarks is to help place the present work among Dr. Hall's philosophical writings and to indicate something of his over-all position. I hope the reader will be led to a serious study of the primary sources, for I am convinced that they constitute one of the major philosophical achievements of our time.

The central problems which occupied Hall were in the realms of the ontology and the epistemology of value. *What Is Value?* deals with the former, and the present work with the latter. These are his two most important books.

1. Dr. Hall died of a sudden heart attack on June 17, 1960.
2. *What Is Value?* (New York: The Humanities Press, and London: Routledge and Kegan Paul, 1952); *Modern Science and Human Values* (Princeton, N.J.: D. van Nostrand Company, 1956); *Philosophical Systems: A Categorial Analysis* (Chicago: University of Chicago Press, 1960).

Modern Science and Human Values is a philosophical study in intellectual history which clarifies, interprets and points up the wider cultural significance of the problems concerning the nature and knowledge of value. *Philosophical Systems* is a study of philosophic method, which is conceived primarily as a clarification and justification of his way of doing philosophy in *What Is Value?* and *Our Knowledge of Fact and Value.* All four works are neatly tied together and form, I feel safe in saying, the most extensive, thorough and perceptive study ever made by one man in the field of value theory.

However, Hall's work should not be thought of as narrowly restricted to the value field. Although he concentrates on the ontology and epistemology of value and on his way of doing philosophy, a wide range of philosophical problems and methods are explored—for example, *Modern Science and Human Values* is an important book in the history and philosophy of science; *What Is Value?* deals with the central ontological problems in the realm of fact as well as in the field of value; *Our Knowledge of Fact and Value* has a carefully worked out, revolutionary epistemology of fact, even though it is conceived as a prolegomenon to his theory of value knowledge; and *Philosophical Systems* is a comparative study of various philosophical approaches, including logical positivism, informal linguistic analysis, phenomenology, existentialism and pragmatism. We might say that these works concern the philosophical enterprise itself and its central metaphysical and epistemological problems. They combine the clarity and rigor of a linguistic analyst and the insight of a profound metaphysician. Whoever is seriously interested in philosophy, regardless of the area of his concern, will find these works richly rewarding.

In trying to indicate something of Hall's over-all position which will be helpful in understanding the work before us, perhaps I should concentrate on his conception of philosophy and its method, for it is on this point that he felt that he was most misunderstood in *What Is Value?* He had a very clear conception of what philosophy is about. This was a matter to which he devoted a great deal of thought. He wrote on it in three different stages of his philosophical development. His essay, "Metaphysics," in *Twentieth Century Philosophy*,[3] was written in his pre-analytic period. His treatment of the problem in "A Categorial Analysis of Value,"[4] in "The 'Proof' of Utility in Bentham and Mill"[5] and in the last chapter of *What Is Value?* was in what may be called his middle period. He then employed a kind of "ideal language" method of formal linguistic analysis similar in some ways to that of the early Wittgenstein. His lecture on "What Is It a Philosopher Does?,"[6] *Philosophical Systems* and the first chapter of the present book constitute his more mature and most extensive discussion of the matter. During this last period he leaned more toward informal linguistic analysis, but he did not feel that he had given up anything essential to the style of *What Is Value?*

Throughout all three periods of his philosophical life, Hall held that philosophy is concerned with getting at the categorial structure of the world. Yet he was bothered by the conflicting claims of rival philosophical systems and how they could be adjudicated in a responsible manner. He did not believe that they could be settled by a straight-

3. Dagobert D. Runes (ed.) (New York: Philosophical Library, 1943).
4. *Philosophy of Science*, XIV (October, 1947), 333-44.
5. *Ethics*, LX (October, 1949), 1-18.
6. Lectures in the Humanities: Thirteenth Series, *University of North Carolina Bulletin*, XXXVII (November, 1957), 5-18.

forward *argumentum ad rem* as in the case of conflicting scientific claims; nor did he believe that they could be settled by rational insight into self-evident truths and deductive procedures. But unlike so many others who shared these convictions, he did not give up on philosophy as a serious cognitive enterprise dealing with significant features or dimensions of both experience and the world. He sought other possibilities in terms of which philosophy could be understood.

He was convinced that in philosophy there is no such thing as either "proof" or "refutation" (in any usual sense) in regard to basic positions. Proof and refutation, he claimed, can be given only within the framework of a philosophical system and thus cannot be given of one's own basic philosophical commitments. Likewise, a refutation of a counter philosophical system would be formulated within one's own. So both proof and refutation would beg the questions at issue. Some of the reviewers of *What Is Value?*, while crediting him with attempting to defend a form of non-naturalism, criticized him for not attempting to refute naturalism and for ignoring naturalistic criticisms of realistic theories of value. In regard to this, he wrote William Frankena: "It seems to me axiomatic that, in ultimate categorial matters (the foundations of a philosophical system), proof and disproof are not only impossible but quite irrelevant—so when it comes to such a basic divergence as that between naturalism and non-naturalism, proof and counter-proof, so far at least as the bases of these standpoints are concerned, become not desiderata but just sources of misunderstanding, confusion and frustration. That is why *What Is Value?* does not indulge in any 'refutations' of naturalism or 'proofs' of objectivism." He then asks the challenging question: "What then is one to do in the strife of systems that constitutes the philosophical enterprise?" And he goes on to say: "The answer is not wholly clear, nor is it outside the strife; but one thing is beyond question—each party has the professional responsibility of clarifying, developing, criticizing, illustratively applying, in short, of 'philosophically analyzing' his basic categories to the very limit of his abilities and tools, and, moreover, of trying to communicate the results to philosophers of other persuasions (in both of which tasks he must, by the nature of the case, finally end in failure)." In unpublished comments on R. M. Hare's review[7] Hall says, "Mr. Hare has not . . . criticized, stated, nor hinted at the major objective of *What Is Value?*—viz., an attempt to state what, supposing there is value, it is. . . . [He] credits the book with an attempt to *defend* the objectivistic standpoint, but this itself is decidedly misleading. A kind of linguistic analysis is finally adopted in it not to defend objectivism but simply to try to state a form of it quite different from those that have been in recent debate, to specify, in brief, in what way value is in the world. . . . Moreover, in the task undertaken the book admittedly ended in failure. The author did not 'fight his way out of the jungle,' and certainly did not come out on the open desert of a study of linguistic usage. His claim, and he probably did not substantiate it, was simply that some light may have been allowed to filter through the tangles of nonnaturalistic positions by the use of the cutting edge of linguistic analysis. However, the new light, if such there was, was on the extra-linguistic problem with which he started—'what is value?' "

It was one of Hall's most fundamental convictions that the only way to get on with philosophy is to operate within a philosophical system and to put it to the test of being fully and rigorously developed in all of its ramifications.

7. *Mind*, LXII (April, 1954), 262-69.

He felt that in so doing one would come to have a sense of its adequacy or inadequacy. But in order to make a responsible comparative judgment about the relative adequacy of several philosophical systems, one would have to work out or try on, so to speak, all of them. In *What Is Value?* he was attempting to clarify and to work out a non-naturalistic value theory. So he discusses dialectically only non-naturalistic proposals. In the present work, he states, clarifies and develops an intentionalistic, empirical theory of knowledge in the realms of both fact and value. He does not attempt to prove the position by arguing against contrary theories. He ignores them. But he was a careful student of all major philosophical positions. He studied them by sympathetically operating within them and criticized them from within. This tolerance was one reason he seemed so tentative about the system he worked out with so much originality and thoroughness. Although he was wedded to his position, he did a good bit of philosophical philandering and divorce was always a distinct possibility. This attitude was grounded in his view of the philosophical enterprise.

However, there is a point not included in this realm of tolerance, namely, the nature of the philosophical enterprise itself. Here he was firm. While willing to experiment with different philosophical systems and to test their adequacy from within, he operated with a common, transcending view of what a philosophical system is and wherein its adequacy lies. He admitted that this commitment is not above the strife of systems, but claimed that it allowed him the greatest *possible* tolerance. In *Philosophical Systems,* contrary to his method elsewhere, he argues dialectically against basic counter-claims, for here he is arguing about the nature of philosophical systems rather than about the nature of whatever it is that a philosophical system is about.

In his early essay on metaphysics, he proposes that metaphysical or philosophical (he there considers metaphysics to embrace ontological, epistemological and axiological problems) theories be tested for adequacy by "applying" them to direct experience. He says, " . . . though our direct experience may be modified to an unascertainable degree by our theories and thus cannot be had 'pure', still we may get around this difficulty by seeking how far it will prove tolerant of modification by our theories. . . . A metaphysical theory should be carefully elaborated and rigorously applied to or read into as much direct experience, and as varied direct experience, as possible. It might well be that as we approximate this, all known metaphysical theories find themselves obstructed somewhere by recalcitrant direct experience. . . . Should we then reject them all. . . ? I would advocate that we select a 'best available at the time' (on the basis of degree of success in reading direct experience in terms of it) and attempt to get on by developing it."[8] In his more mature view, he looks more to the grammar of everyday speech than to direct experience, for he maintains that it embodies our "natural" categories or primary analyses of the world. But he does not let appeal to ordinary language completely replace recourse to direct experience. "It is," he says, "the grammar of common sense, combined, as I have suggested, with the structure of our unsophisticated experience, which most generally actually functions as that which is given to philosophers of different persuasions, however little they may acknowledge this common ground even to themselves."[9] So his final conclusion would be that every philosophical system must be tested for adequacy by fully developing it and by seeing how much of ordinary dis-

8. *Twentieth Century Philosophy*, p. 186.
9. *Philosophical Systems*, p. 157.

course and unsophisticated experience can be read in terms of the proposed categorial system without doing violence to either. The result is categorial knowledge about the world, which consists of neither rationalistic, nor empirical, nor analytic truths in any ordinary sense. It is *sui generis*.

In *Modern Science and Human Values,* Hall unravels the modern development of a value-free mode of scientific thought and thus the clear distinction between the realms of fact and value. He also traces the uncertain and frustrating efforts of modern man in the age of science to achieve an understanding of values. He believes that the distinction and separation of the two realms is a sound approach, but that our fundamental cultural problem consists of our apparent inability to understand what values are and to develop fruitful ways of obtaining value knowledge. "Western man today," he says in the conclusion of the book, "has achieved an exceedingly powerful tool for discovering facts and factual laws. He has done this by ridding himself, in this procedure, of value thinking. He has attained nothing comparable in the area of value, although he has made some progress here in clearing his mind of factual thinking. If he can cling to the conviction that there are values in the world until he can work out a reliable technique for discovering them concretely, he may survive. Otherwise he will be forced down the path to complete value skepticism. Such skepticism involves no logical inconsistency, but it stands in contradiction to man's whole nature and outlook. I doubt whether he can remake himself sufficiently to live with it, and I certainly would hate to see him try."

In *What Is Value?,* Hall attempts to clarify what values are and how they are objectively in the world. He contends that value is neither a property nor a relation, whether natural or non-natural, but a way in which particulars and

properties (or relations) are "related." "Value," he says,"
is the oughting-to-exemplify or the it-were-good-to-exempli-
fy that obtains between a particular or particulars and a
quality or relation (analogously to fact, which is the actual
exemplification of a quality or relation by a particular or by
particulars)" (p. 226). Thus he contends that the nature
of value and how it is in the world are shown by the structure of "ought" sentences.

In the present work, he develops a theory of knowledge
which is empirical and yet avoids skepticism in the realms
both of fact and of value. It will, I think, make his value
realism more acceptable to our age. If heeded, it could
work a revolution in our patterns of philosophical thought
and have far-reaching cultural consequences.

I said in the beginning that this was Hall's last work.
It is the last that he completed. However, he had outlined
in great detail a proposed book in aesthetics. His notes
on this subject, as well as a volume of his papers and es-
says, may be developed and published.

Publication of this book has been made possible by a
grant from the University of North Carolina Research
Council and by a grant of the Ford Foundation under its
program for assisting American university presses in the
publication of works in the humanities and the social
sciences.

E. M. ADAMS

Chapel Hill, N.C.

Our Knowledge of Fact and Value

I

The Linguistic Approach

IN EVERY undertaking it is of first importance to start right. This is particularly true in philosophy, but it is also particularly difficult in this subject. At the beginning we not only lack achieved results; we are also in want of accepted criteria of success. The best an author can do is to appeal to faith, to ask his readers to go along with him to the end and then judge what he has offered them, whether it be fruit or dry leaves.

We shall start from common sense and continue with our feet always placed on that firm ground. One might even characterize the position to be explored as that of "common-sense realism"; certainly it is in many ways close to the standpoint of the great Scottish advocate of common sense, Thomas Reid, though not as it is frequently described. In what follows there will be no preachment to philosophers to give up their fine distinctions and metaphysical speculations in favor of ordinary occupations in the market place or on the farm; nor any attempt to elevate some supposedly universal beliefs of the "man on the street" into an epistemology or ontology. The ordinary man in his ordinary affairs is not called upon to do philosophy nor does he maintain any philosophical position in a professional sense. Nevertheless we shall be driven back to him —not so much to *what* he thinks directly about matters of philosophical concern as to *how* he thinks about his own enterprises, so far as these involve commitments that have bearing on philosophical issues.

The reason for this is a fact and an interpretation.

The fact to which I refer is the unending, or in any case the unended, controversy between philosophical schools. Each thinks itself the correct and the only correct theory, and many claim the power to prove themselves so. This is disconcerting since they contradict one another, asserting that only bodies exist and that mind alone does, that reality is many and that it is one, and so on. In a certain sense each is justified in its contention, for within the framework of its own categories and methods its rivals do appear foolish and wholly unacceptable. The trouble is that this is true for each, therefore for all, so that which one you individually accept turns out to be for the most part accidental. Consequently, if we are to evaluate these competitors intelligently it seems necessary to get an outside and impartial standpoint or criterion, and this I find in the modes of thought, the "categories," as I call them, of everyday life. Such categories involve commitments some of which no doubt reveal the influence of particular schools of thought, but even these have stood the test of use in everyday life and absorption into everyday thinking and are thus to that extent neutralized in the strife of systems.

The interpretation I referred to concerns the philosophical undertaking itself—what it is a philosopher does when he is about his proper business. My contention is that, although the philosopher is seeking a sort of knowledge about the world, including himself, this knowledge is not empirical in character—it is not the result of, nor can it be properly tested by, specific observations, no matter how numerous, subtle and reflexive. Indeed, if his knowledge were of the empirical kind, it would be hard to understand why philosophical controversy, at least on some issues, had not been settled centuries ago. What the philosopher wants is a knowledge of the "basic dimensions" of the world (to use my terminology), the "essence" (to put it Platonically) of existence, knowledge and value, an appropriate set of "categories" (to borrow from Aristotle), whose propriety is not a matter of expediency or of emotional satisfaction but of insight into the kind of universe we are in. Take existence. We think of houseflies, tempera, toothaches, politicians, typhoons as existing at some time or other; but not so of prince-charmings, air-castles, centaurs, a largest finite positive integer. The former, it is presumed, have something in common the latter lack. What is it (their existence)?

This interpretation of philosophy makes sense of the fact mentioned earlier. Philosophical controversies seem to be and perhaps are interminable since the most reliable and foolproof method of settling disputes, namely that of empirical science, is not available for their resolution; by their nature they are about all-pervading matters, including themselves. Through what telescope or microscope would we look, what readings of what recording instruments could we consult, to determine whether Aristotle or Berkeley is correct? In this situation I find myself driven to the tacit, undeveloped, frequently clashing modes and categories of everyday thought, primarily as these are discovered in everyday language, for a criterion of the soundness of rival philosophies, on the simple assumption that this is the best we can do. The high a priori road is all right within certain philosophical systems, such as Descartes', but cannot decide between them—for example, between Descartes' and Hume's; the low empirical path is fine for science but is not germane to philosophy. The knowledge we seek is indeed neither a priori nor empirical. However, it would be a mistake to suppose that there are only two kinds of knowledge and that if neither is available to the philosopher then he must give up the attempt to know reality and turn to the insight which this giving up gives—an outcome which seems to me to be just a latter-day form of skepticism.

It is my contention that there is a third kind of knowledge which I can do little more than name at the present stage. I call it "categorial" and find its test in the main forms of everyday thought about everyday matters in so far as these reveal commitment in some tacit way to a view or perhaps several views about how the world is made up, about its basic "dimensions." We find these forms of everyday thought chiefly in the grammatical structures (in a broad sense) of daily speech, in what may be called the resources of ordinary language, although they are also present in the ways we personally experience things, for the latter reflect, to a great extent, the formative influence of our mother tongue.

So now we have a criterion, in some loose sense, by which to judge our undertaking. Have we any justification of it, or is its choice completely arbitrary? Certainly we have no proof, in any logical sense, but there are considerations that can be brought to bear.

In the first place, our criterion is objective as between clashing philosophical systems. True, it is not as objective in its sphere as science is in its own. But it is better than no general criterion at all, or than criteria borrowed from and peculiar to some particular philosophy or to the insights of some individual thinker. And of course science itself cannot furnish final grounds for decision between rival philosophies, since it is not sufficiently inclusive in its interests (omitting, for example, the whole region of values) and is, indeed, hardly more than a specialization of common sense as it searches for regularities.

Moreover, common sense is the actual meeting ground of all divergent philosophical viewpoints. Not only do all philosophers pay it lip service; they all come back to common speech to give substance to their technical jargon. Their attenuations are derived from the crude expressions of everyday. As a matter of fact, philosophers could not communicate their ideas to novices or debate their contentions with one another unless somewhere they "descended" to a language common to all. This does not mean they cannot build upon it; what is implied is that, however magnificent the superstructure, it must be suitable to its foundations and thus in some degree reveal their character.

Perhaps I am doing little more than pleading for honesty. Philosophers do seem in practice to fall back on my criterion. Few if any have been able to face with equanimity the accusation that their particular view leads logically to the denial of other minds or centers of experience, to the reduction, for example, of others' sufferings to one's own hearing of groans and seeing of grimaces. Why? Not because such solipsism is illogical, but, I submit, because it is so foreign to our everyday modes of thought.

Certainly there are objections to our test; I mention two which are, perhaps, the most serious.

First, as we shall see before long and could in any event anticipate, the grammar of everyday language does not on every philosophical issue give a clear and unambiguous decision. It frequently needs "clarification" and, indeed, correction. How can this be? Have we then some further grounds, some really ultimate criterion? I think not. Common sense is critical of itself. For example, it demands self-consistency. This explains the intolerability of the so-called logical paradoxes, which are contradictions arising from everyday ways of thinking when these are pushed in certain directions, as when one speaks of classes whose members are classes, or of words or sentences which can refer to themselves. Let me cite one case. Jevons' paradox arises as follows: On a card one reads, "The sentence on the other side is true," but turning the card one finds, "The sentence on the other side is false." If the first is true, then it is false, whereas if it is false, then it is true (assuming that "It is false that the sentence on the other side is false" means the same as "The sentence on the other side is true"). My point is that it is common sense itself that rejects such an outcome and forces us to reconsider whether and when a sentence can be allowed to refer to itself, and, moreover, holds us back from a wholesale prohibition of self-reference which would deny us, for example, the opportunity of asserting that all propositions are either true or false.

Second, different languages have different grammars as well as vocabularies. Are we to trust English or even Indo-European languages for our inventory of the common modes of thought embedded in everyday life?

Let me illustrate by an example drawn not from my philosophy but from that of Descartes. *Cogito ergo sum.* Since I am thinking, even in carrying through the method of universal doubt, I must exist. This seems all right in Latin or French or English, but will it do in Japanese? I understand that Japanese has over twenty expressions that could be translated "I," each with its special and appropriate use. The "I" may refer to one as a friend or a stranger to the hearer, a social superior or inferior, and so on. Which one is proved to exist by Descartes' argument? Are the others left without proven existence? Or does the argument establish the existence of different selves in different situations? Does it perhaps prove a male self's existence but not a female's? Could it never be applied to and by the Japanese emperor (I understand he has his own exclusive personal pronoun)? Perhaps there is a special type of scholarly situation in which the recluse, talking only to himself, has an appropriate designation for himself? If so, then is that the only ego Descartes was able to prove exists? When he mixed with the crowds in the streets of Amsterdam, did he have to lay aside the certitude of his existence?

Moreover, I understand that in most situations involving doing or experiencing something on the part of the speaker, descriptions in Japanese tend to omit the subject— the activity is stated by itself without specifically ascribing it to anyone. Does this mean that if Descartes had thought and written in Japanese his logic could never have given him his basic certainty, for instead of "I think, therefore I am" he would have had something like "Doubting, in a lonely room, by a warm stove"? To the Japanese mind uncontaminated by the academic traditions of Western philosophy, is it necessary, in order that thinking occur, that there be a thinker?

I have no final answer to this type of challenge. The approach to philosophy taken in the present study does involve the assumption that mankind as a whole has a modicum of common modes of thought, that there are categories to which we are all more or less committed and that these are discernible in everyday speech. Perhaps advances in linguistic anthropology will force the abandonment of this assumption. In the meantime, however, it is worth a try to see what we can do if the assumption be allowed. My conviction, though perhaps it amounts to little more than faith at this point, is that every language is intentional, that is, is about matters that are extra-linguistic, and that it uses both descriptive and evaluative devices in speaking about them. This premise will be amply illustrated by typical cases drawn from ordinary English; to what extent other languages may give it the lie is an issue beyond the project here undertaken.[1]

1. It goes without saying that the cases are presented not as forming a good inductive sample but as possibly leading to insights into what is so obvious as to be ordinarily neglected. The reader who is interested in the methodological assumptions of the present chapter might find it profitable to look at my *Philosophical Systems: a Categorial Analysis* (Chicago: University of Chicago Press, 1960).

2

An Intentionalistic Empiricism

THE ACCOUNT of knowledge in the present book is in one sense in the empiricist tradition. It assumes that all our knowledge is based upon particular experiences. Of course we generalize upon these experiences and thereby formulate factual laws in science, moral rules in normative ethics, and critical canons in art. But such generalizations find their evidence, in the last analysis, in individual experiences.

This not only agrees with the main tradition in Anglo-American philosophy; it is also in harmony with the criterion of everyday modes of speech mentioned in the preceding chapter. Let me in this connection simply point out the finality in ordinary thought of such expressions as "I saw it with my own eyes," "Look for yourself," and so on, when the matter is one of fact, or "Can't you feel it?," "Don't you want it?," when it is one of value. Of course we make mistakes in either region, sometimes seeing things that are not there (in dreams and hallucinations) or again desiring things we should not have (in moments of impetuosity). Both errors will have to be dealt with later, and the ever-present possibility of their occurrence will force us to give up any claim to certainty in our knowledge. They will not, however, require us to cast aside the concrete experiences people actually have as the most reliable bases of knowledge available to us.

In another way, however, the empiricism here to be

developed is out of keeping with the traditional form of this philosophy. It breaks with that tradition precisely at the point where that broke with the proprieties of everyday English. Basically, our ordinary language is about things and events in the world outside us. When on occasion we do talk of our inner experiences, our speech reveals, characteristically, that the experiences are themselves outwardly directed. Let us look into this more concretely.

The English noun "experience" is just the Anglican form of the present participle of the Latin verb "experiri," meaning to try, to put to the test. Thus originally "experience" signified trying, testing, experimenting. It was a form of a transitive verb of action, involving doing something with or to something.

Most of our cognitive terms in English have had a similar source. "Perception" came from a verb signifying to *lay hold of* or *seize*. We still, of course, have the literal meaning of physical activity in "grasping," "comprehending," "apprehending." One can "catch" a fleeting idea or a high-flying ball, "grapple" with a proof or an assailant, "capture" a thought or a criminal. It would be going too far to assert that all cognitive terms in our language have had this ancestry, but what is significant is that many of them have and that "experience" finds itself at home with these. This is a first step towards seeing that "experience" belongs to the same family, that it primarily connotes a mode of referring rather than a form of occurring.

But now this line of approach easily leads to the pragmatic error that knowing is itself just a species of doing (in a literal, not a metaphorical, sense). Good English usage is against this identification. Cognitive verbs, and cognitive uses of verbs that may also be used to express physical activity, have certain peculiarities that mark them off from action-words used literally.

In the first place, the activity expressed by a cognitive verb is unique because, although it is directed upon an object, it does not make sense to suppose that anything is done to the object by this action. One can "grasp" a toy balloon or the proof of a theorem. It is relevant to ask, "What happened to the balloon?," but not "What happened to the proof?," as a result of one's grasping it. Suppose one perceives a soap-bubble; if this is one's whole act upon it, it is improper to look for any consequences upon the object. However, if one seizes it literally it is quite within the proprieties of language to try to observe the effects on the bubble. If I kick you, I am apt to hurt you, but not if I merely think of you, however unkind my thoughts.

Originally, in the history of human thought, this distinction may have arisen from actual observation. Certain primitive peoples, we are told, firmly believed that just thinking of someone, imagining him in one's mind, might have a profound effect upon him, perhaps transporting him with lightning-like speed from a distance to the immediate vicinity. Perhaps some genius discovered by careful observation that this was not so. But however the distinction arose, it is now deep-rooted in our language, so deep that a break with it is treated not as a sign of poor powers of observation but as a meaningless utterance.

We smile when Johnny, coming home from school with very red ears, explains the fact by saying that his teacher must be thinking of him; we take a more serious view of the matter, however, when he admits that his teacher saw him pull Susan's hair, for we surmise that his ears got a boxing.

Seeing something, then, or hearing it or thinking about it is not doing anything to it—this is in our present culture a matter of using language correctly. This is why most of us treat psychokinesis as disrespectable: to say that we looked at the dice and concentrated upon them does not warrant any inference that we may have causally affected their antics, and we think it rather silly to put this to statistical test.

If something has happened to the object, if it has been marred or moved or otherwise maltreated, we know, without investigation, that someone or something did more than barely notice it. Indeed, a universal test of physical action is that the object has been affected by it in some way. Another test is that someone observe the action itself.

This brings us to a second difference. Concerning a person's alleged overt behavior, we can always sensibly ask, "Who saw him do it?" Not so for his cognitive acts. Here again the distinction may have arisen from observation; in fact, there are those today who claim that the difference is not empirically sound, that we can literally pry into other people's consciousness and see them see or hear them hear or in some peculiar way watch them think about something. But such a claim seems odd and superstitious precisely because the inability to perceive another's cognitive acts is so firmly built into our language-framework.

Of course, it is perfectly permissible to say, "I saw you look at him," but that what is referred to is the physical act is indicated by the fact that no incongruity arises when the words, "out of the corners of your eyes," are added. We do sometimes talk as though we observed others perceiving things or thinking about them, yet I believe we can attribute this peculiarity to a lazy or metaphorical way of speaking, as witnessed by the legitimacy of such challenges as, "I saw you look right at me; didn't you see me?," "He noticed she was listening intently and wondered whether she heard his slip of the tongue," "I observed him look at the page for a full half hour but later learned that he was so distracted that he didn't see a word on it." So I think that when we say we see others see or hear things, what we mean is that we see them take characteristic postures of looking or listening, not that we literally see them see or hear.

And, as if this were not queer enough, consider how we talk about our own cognitive acts. Suppose that I claim that I saw someone in a hotel lobby, and suppose furthermore that you doubt it. I certainly would not try to back my assertion by saying that I saw myself see him or heard myself do it or otherwise perceived myself perceive him. Of course, it does sound all right to affirm that I can remember my seeing him; but if you are persistent I will have to admit that my memory is very fallible. In any case, how can one remember unless one had an original experience to be remembered? It is this primary cognitive act we want to observe. Looking to my ordinary ways of speaking I find I would answer your challenge in one or both of two ways. One is to describe my physical behavior. I might tell you, "Well you see, I came in this door and was walking toward that table when I lifted my eyes for a moment toward the stairway on the right—I don't quite know why—and there I saw him." The other is to describe the object seen: "I tell you I saw him right by the stairway. He was wearing a dark suit with a blue and gray striped tie and kept glancing about the lobby as though afraid of being recognized."

In neither of these cases do I describe my act of seeing this gentleman. In the second form of response, I would be characterizing not my act but its object. In the first, I would be specifying some accompanying physical acts which might occur without my noticing the gentleman in question at all, that is, literally without my seeing him.

But if you challenge me further, "Did you actually notice him, were you aware of his being there?," I would be either mystified or annoyed; I would probably answer,

"Who is in any better position to say than I?" I have put this as a personal conjecture about what I might do; actually I want you to consider it a statement of what I conceive everyday English to allow me to say. It certainly does not permit me to use the expression, "I see myself seeing him," and even "I notice my seeing him" is questionable. Now, some philosophers may introduce at this point talk about introspection as a special sort of seeing, a seeing within. I do not wish to argue against them but only to point out that this sort of language is not idiomatic in everyday English and to report that, when philosophers who use it distinguish clearly between our acts of cognition on the one hand and, on the other, both our accompanying bodily behavior and the object upon which the act is directed, they usually come out with a description of the act as "transparent," "diaphanous," or otherwise very close to being unobservable.

I must leave this point for the present. All I have tried to show is that, following good English usage, just as it is wrong to speak of acts of knowing as doing anything to their objects, so it is improper to talk this way about seeing, hearing, touching or otherwise perceiving them, save possibly in some difficult and perhaps esoteric sense. So again we are led to oppose any easy pragmatic identification of knowing with doing.

But now we come to the most pronounced difference of all. Cognitive verbs can take not only nouns but also substantival clauses, and infinitive and participial phrases, as objective complements. A common case and one perhaps most easily analyzed is a clause introduced by "that" as a subordinating conjunction. I may see a man and I may see that he is bald; although I am permitted (linguistically, that is) to strike him, I cannot strike that he is bald. I am allowed to feel the board and to feel that it is rough;

I can sandpaper the board only, I must not sandpaper that it is rough.

It might be thought, upon first consideration, that "hearing" is different from other cognitive verbs, especially verbs expressing sensory perception, in this respect. But if there is a difference I think it is one of degree only. I admit that such expressions as "I hear that your father has a bad cough" and "I hear that the second violin was off key" mean to state another person's report, not one's own auditory perception, but we are allowed to say, "I hear your father coughing" and "I can hear that the second violin is slightly off key." And something similar is true of "seeing." When one says, "I see that Mr. Wilson's hair is white," one may be reporting an item in a newspaper one has read or, on the other hand, one's own direct visual perception.

When we come to more abstract cognitive terms, such as "knowing," "believing," "thinking," we find that English usage is even more complicated. "I believe Mr. Coughlin" means that I believe what Mr. Coughlin has said. "I know Mr. Coughlin" means that I am directly acquainted with him, have seen him and can recognize him. But all these subtleties and variations may be put aside for our present purpose. The simple point is that cognitive verbs can take as objective complements clauses and phrases which can be made into independent sentences themselves by suitable modification of their verbal constituents. As an example, consider the sentence, "I presume that he has met our president." Here we can eliminate the "that" without a change of meaning. Then we have the clause "he has met our president" immediately after "I presume" and serving as its object. Lift it from this context and it is a perfectly good sentence in its own right.

This is not true of verbs expressing ordinary physical action; they must always take nouns or pronouns, never "sentences," that is, substantival clauses, as objects. Let us investigate what this implies.

An ordinary English sentence in the indicative mood asserts a fact (or if generalized, a set of facts). This is perhaps the best way of stating what a fact is, namely, that it is that which is asserted by a true, affirmative, indicative sentence. The fact that I have a sheet of paper before me is precisely what is affirmed by the sentence, "I have a sheet of paper before me." Facts are fragile; try to modify one and you find you have destroyed it, have replaced it by another. Change anything about the fact that I have a sheet of paper before me—put the paper behind me, crumple it so that it is no longer a sheet, replace the paper by a book—and the original fact is exterminated. This is not true of an individual thing (still going by the grammar of everyday English). It has many accidents (in Aristotle's sense) any of which can be modified without destroying it. The sheet of paper can be written upon, given to a student, placed in a desk without being destroyed.

This is related to what we noticed earlier. Cognitive acts do nothing to their objects. We now see that, when their objects are facts, they could do nothing to them other than to annihilate them utterly. My thinking or perceiving that a man is bald cannot modify that fact, cannot leave an impression on it, so to speak, as the mark of its having occurred. But individual things can be changed without destruction. So it is quite permissible to look for some modification which any action upon them may have produced.

In this connection I want to turn our attention to a very commonplace but nevertheless, when you stop to think of it, a most amazing characteristic of indicative sentences. They may be true or again false, and in either case equally they say something, are meaningful. Let us concentrate for the moment on false sentences. A false, affirmative, indicative sentence asserts a fact that does not obtain, that simply is not in the universe at all, and yet the sentence is significant. This is astonishing, as though one were pointing at nothing, at emptiness. But I am not suggesting that we stop and gape at this phenomenon, nor, at the present stage, that we attempt to analyze it (clearly the pointing analogy is wrong).

What I want to do is to fit it into our account of cognitive verbs and thereby to show how odd are the "acts" which they express.

A cognitive verb with a substantival clause as objective complement may be taken, then, to refer to an act whose object is a fact or a "non-fact," that is, a fact that does not obtain.

Let us consider the latter case. Suppose the dependent clause, if made into a sentence in its own right, to be false. The whole sentence then could be true and in any case it would be meaningful. That is, it would be meaningful and perhaps true to affirm an "act" upon an object not existing at all!

Take an example. "He believes that he left his umbrella in the hall." This sentence may be true even though "He left his umbrella in the hall" is false. Suppose that the latter *is* false. The whole sentence then meaningfully and perhaps truly asserts an act (that of his believing that he left his umbrella in the hall) directed upon an object that simply is not in the universe. A completely similar analysis would hold for, "She thinks that her husband is working late at his office."

We now, I trust, can see how different mental or cognitive acts must be from ordinary physical ones, since they do nothing to their objects, appear to be almost if not entirely unobservable and can be directed upon objects that do not exist at all.

There is, then, a sufficiently striking dissimilarity in everyday English between cognitive verbs and verbs of ordinary action to justify rejecting that form of pragmatism which says that knowing is a kind of doing; if it is to be called an action at all, it must be immediately noted that it is a strange kind of activity indeed. It is so odd that perhaps we ought to refuse to call it an activity. This, however, would probably be too radical, especially as we should praise the pragmatist for an insight never attained by the British empiricist, namely, that experience is an activity, not an inert stuff. But this is a bad way to state it, and I beg leave to formulate the idea in my somewhat more linguistic fashion.

"Experiencing" as a verb shares all the characteristics of cognitive verbs, with their affinity in some respects to verbs of action in the proper sense and their striking dissimilarities in others. We have seen that it has a common ancestral trait, being derived from a term that strictly referred to a physical action. Moreover, it is transitive; it demands an object. One never simply experiences; one always experiences something—the sunset, a regret, some reward for a good deed done, the effects of a hasty decision. It is true that in the passive voice or again as a noun it is occasionally put in an absolute construction, as when one says, "He is a man of political experience," or "She was experienced in the wiles of her sex." I do not think, however, that it is in these relatively infrequently occurring usages that the term is taken by our empiricist friends. In the main, absolute constructions using the word associate with the sense of being skilled or having an ability arising from repeatedly doing something and have little if anything to do with the "ideas" of Locke or the "perceptions" of Hume.[1]

"Experiencing" is also like cognitive verbs in not implying any modification of its object owing to the activity it marks. Noticing a fly crawling along the ceiling or thinking about a square root does not entail any observable effect upon the object, and likewise neither does experiencing a sunset over the Pacific Ocean or the cold water of Lake Superior in June.

Moreover, "experiencing" sometimes takes a subordinate clause or an equivalent (such as a participial or infinitive phrase), as contrasted with a noun or pronoun, as its objective complement. I may have experienced a sudden fright or being deserted by all my friends, a whiff of honeysuckle or that enjoyment is enhanced by its previous absence, a pleasant memory or that students often dislike a professor because of his aloofness. One is linguistically permitted to experience that seasickness is misery, the Pacific Ocean is very wide and one can get the best steak dinners right at home.

As these cases seem to indicate, "experience" with a verbal expression in its objective complement usually carries the suggestion of repetition, of a principle or regularity discovered personally, whereas if one wishes to speak of a single experience, the verb is used with a noun. If this is true, it is an interesting fact, but not one that invalidates

1. Locke, for example, introduces Book II, which is about ideas, as follows: "*Idea is the object of thinking.* Every man being conscious to himself that he thinks, and that which his mind is applied about whilst thinking, being the ideas that are there, it is past doubt that men have in their minds several ideas, such as those expressed by the words whiteness, hardness, sweetness, thinking, motion, man, elephant, army, drunkenness, and others" (*An Essay Concerning Human Understanding,* Book II, Chapter I, Section 1). This does not explicitly deny that ideas are referential, but it does invite the interpretation that they are semantically self-enclosed, being the objects of an act of thinking, not themselves such acts.

my main contention, that as a verb "experience" can take a clause or its equivalent as an object, and thus is similar to such words as "know," "perceive" and "see."

It might be contended that the substantival form of our word has uses which do not fit our intentionalistic interpretation. Consider "I've just had the most harrowing experience," "Most of our everyday experience is humdrum," "His experience that day changed his whole life." These seem to be about events without any suggestion of a reference in them to anything further, such as physical fact. They clearly are about events, and we must not deny that experiences are occurrences people do undergo. But suppose we wish to get a specification of the experiences alluded to. This, I contend, would eventually lead to a characterization of them in terms of their objects, of what they are about: the harrowing experience, perhaps, was of an automobile accident in which someone was killed; the humdrum experiences of everyday are of crowds of people in stores or subways, of unexciting food and uninteresting television shows and the like; the crucial experience may have been of a great work of art or a moving address by an eminent thinker.

I have been arguing that the grammar of "experience" in everyday English puts it with cognitive terms; experience is semantical, referential, always about something. This is what I mean by saying that it is intentional. It is the tendency to ignore, if not explicitly to deny, that intentionalism that I want to oppose in traditional British empiricism. Naturally their very language opposes the philosophers of this persuasion. Locke, Berkeley, Hume, James Mill all use terms for the elements of experience which, in the vernacular, are referential or intentional in significance —such words as "ideas," "perceptions," "sensations," "feelings." They try to purify them of all semantical connotation but the taint remains and can be detected by anyone sensitive to the little things that give language its flavor, like the prepositional phrases that modify these nouns or the habits of their verbal counterparts to take objective complements.[2]

The question naturally arises, why did these men attempt to break with the grammar of their native tongue? I think the answer is not difficult to come by or particularly open to controversy. They thought of themselves as setting up a science of the mind (of "human understanding" or of "moral subjects" as they put it) on the model of Newtonian physics, and in their enthusiasm for the new project did not pay sufficient attention to the marks of mental phenomena, which are cognitive whereas physical occurrences are not.

The task before us, then, is to make an empirical analysis of our knowledge of fact and value, but one that, by contrast with British empiricism, will remain true to the intentionalism of everyday thought and language.

It will be contended in the second part of this book that our value-claims are more complex than our assertions of fact, that they include the latter in a peculiar way. This being so, it is proper to start with an analysis of our knowl-

2. Let me give an example, drawn from Locke (with my italics). "Whence has [the mind] all the materials of reason and knowledge? To this I answer in one word, from *experience*. . . . Our *observation* employed either *about* external sensible objects, or *about* the internal operations of our minds, perceived and reflected on by ourselves, is that which supplies our understandings with all the materials of thinking. . . . First, our senses, conversant *about* particular sensible objects, do convey into the mind several distinct perceptions *of* things, according to those various ways wherein those objects do affect them. . . ." Second, "But as I call the other Sensation, so I call this Reflection, the ideas it affords being such only as the mind gets by reflecting *on* its own operations within itself. By reflection . . . I . . . mean that notice which the mind takes *of* its own operations, and the manner of them; by reason whereof there come to be ideas *of* these operations in the understanding" (*Human Understanding*, Book II, Chapter I, Sections 2, 3, 4).

edge of fact. Our concern will be with its foundation-walls, leaving the superstructure to logicians and philosophers of science. That basis, as I have said, is the totality of actual, particular sensory perceptions.

To avoid a possible misapprehension, we should pause for a moment to answer a hypothetical objection. "I thought you made the forms of everyday speech and conception your basis," says the objector, "but now you appear to have turned to sensory perceptions." My response is that we have here two different groundings. One is the support to be found for the whole philosophical system here presented. It is to perform this function that I brought in the grammar of ordinary language. The other is intrasystemic, the factual basis of knowledge as interpreted within that structure. This I placed in the totality of actually occurring sensory perceptions.

But now a more serious objection may arise. Is the basing of our knowledge of fact upon concrete perceptions in accord with common thought and speech?

I think it is, as I have already intimated. I must admit, however, that I have personally been influenced by two other considerations as well. One is the amazing success in our modern world of the empirical sciences, the sciences based on sensory observations. By "success" here I refer mainly to their ability to find regularities upon which verifiable predictions can be grounded. Indulgence in speculation and flights of imagination on the part of great scientific geniuses may have contributed to the process of discovering the laws of nature, but these laws are themselves established only to the degree to which they are verified by perceptions (or, perhaps more strictly formulated, to the degree to which cohering sets of them have been found to agree with observations). These sciences use logical deductions, but never accept them as, *by themselves,* sufficient to establish any factual knowledge.

The reverse of the coin is that the very experts in the a priori, namely the logicians and mathematicians, have, by and large, given up all claims in their sciences to the acquisition of knowledge of fact. They simply draw out the consequences of the postulates and definitions with which they start. And however plausible and even self-evident these starting-points may seem, if they contain factual assertions they are subject to check and perhaps rejection by the empirical sciences: witness the giving up of Euclidean geometry by recent physics.

But these are only reinforcements or extensions of what I find to be "common sense." I admit that the average person is gullible, loves to rest content with authority, not bothering to find out for himself. But we are all in the position of needing to supplement our own perceptions by those of others. And if the average man accepts miracles and special revelations as reported by others, this is because he thinks that the others have actually seen the events or heard the voices. Nothing is, in principle, more conclusive than "seeing it with one's own eyes" or "hearing it with one's own ears," as we say, when the question is one of fact.

Of course perception is not infallible. We sometimes do see visions, hear "voices," suffer sundry hallucinations. But the veridicality of these experiences is questioned precisely because they are in disagreement with other sensory experience or with regularities of perceived events extrapolated to cover the cases in question. In modifying the British tradition by recognizing that all experience is active or referential, we made unavailable the argument for incorrigibility resting on the assumption that perceptions are simply events. Sheer events cannot of course be corrected, but neither are they correct, so that this is not a serious loss if one wants a maximum of cognitive security. But it cannot be denied that our kind of empirical intentionalism has no place for certainty. It does, however, offer probability, as will be shown in Chapter 7.

Part I. Our Knowledge of Fact

3

The Language of Perception

EXPERIENCE is always "of" something; perceptions refer, make claims, are veridical or illusory. This is what I shall mean when speaking of perceptions as sentences, as forming a "natural" language of the mind to be contrasted with conventional languages of physical things (whether mounds of ink or emissions of sound).

I think that the scholastics and Aristotle himself so thought of perceptions, but right at the start we must avoid a mistake of "The Philosopher" which was eventually corrected, but only after it had left seeds that were to grow into future brambles. Aristotle apparently supposed that the written sign stood for, that is, referred to the spoken, and the spoken, the mental. He was wrong in both cases, for all three (the written, spoken and mental signs) stand for the thing itself.[1] When you ask a friend in a letter, "Has the weather been good there?" you are not asking about the sounds you might have uttered had he been present and you had phrased your question orally, or about your state of mind—or, for that matter, about your friend's utterances or states of mind. You are asking, as you would have asked orally and as, no doubt, you are asking in your mind, about the weather at your friend's location.

Of course it is always possible to use signs to refer to other signs; but then the character of these signs (written, spoken, mental) is irrelevant. There is only one restriction

1. Of course not every isolated word is a sign of something.

to this generalization; it seems that we can never perceive perceptions or other mental signs. However, we can think about them as well as write about them and talk about them. Perceptions form our natural, unconventional language. They contain claims about the physical world only. They never refer to other signs *as* signs, but only as physical events or things. It is true that we sometimes say, "I perceive what you mean," or "He has a perceptive mind," but such uses are definitely metaphorical.

In the system here being developed, the final basis of our knowledge of fact is our natural language of sensory perception. This, however, must be supplemented by conventional language, partly because we do have some factual knowledge of our perceptions themselves whereas, as just pointed out, we do not perceive them, and partly because we could not get beyond them to many things we wish to accomplish in our knowledge of fact, especially to generalizations upon them, without the aid of conventional sentences.

Before going further, perhaps we had better pause on some terminological matters. To speak of perceptions as "sentences" and perceptual experience as a "natural language" is somewhat extraordinary and is hardly justifiable by reference to common idiom. This terminology must be set down as a philosophical idiosyncrasy, but one which serves a purpose. That purpose is to accentuate the semantical character of perceptions, already emphasized in the previous chapter in speaking of the intentional character of experience generally. Even more specifically, perceptions, like sentences, are true or false. If it be objected that only veridical perceptions are called "perceptions," that we refer to mistakes at this level as "distortions" or "illusions" or "hallucinations," I would agree. "He perceived (or saw) that there was a dog in the yard" functions more like "He knew that there was a dog in the yard" than like "He asserted that there was a dog in the yard," for it ordinarily implies "There was a dog in the yard."   In this respect, we do not have in ordinary speech a good analogue for the noun, "sentence," or for the verbs, "state," "assert," "say."   If we wish to claim that his experience was erroneous, we use such circumlocutions as "He thought he saw that there was a dog in the yard" or "He imagined that there was a dog in the yard," but these forms of expression suggest that his experience was different from that of seeing or perceiving.   If we want to speak only of the experience itself and leave out any claim on our part concerning its veridicalness or illusoriness, we lack a neutral terminology analogous to "sentence" or to "asserts."   Still, it is only common sense to admit that we sometimes misperceive, and so the analogy with statement and misstatement, with true and false assertion is warranted.

The noun "imagination" and the verb "imagine" are sometimes used primarily to express the speaker's conviction of the erroneousness of the experience mentioned, as in "That business of finding a snake in his bed was all a matter of John's imagination" and "She just imagined that he was watching her."   On the other hand, these words frequently mean to point out experiences different in kind from perception, supposing that the person having them is not "taken in" by them.   This is particularly true when the idea of the creative or artistic is associated with their use. Here the metaphor of natural language helps.   We can think of these cases as sentences whose assertion is suspended.   Think of descriptions in works of fiction.   They have all the marks of ordinary declarative statements except that they are embedded in a fictional context.   We do not speak or think of them as false; they simply are not to be taken seriously as assertions of fact.   Their assertiveness is suspended by their context. Something similar is true of the processes of creative imagination. They are as truly about things as are ordinary perceptions, yet they are not erroneous, like illusions or hallucinations. We do not, except under extraordinary conditions, imagine images; we imagine scenes and incidents and people doing this or that. Yet the difference from perceiving these things is that in creative imagination we recognize that the "perceptions" are all fictive. Of course such imaginings do not form part of the empirical basis of our knowledge of fact.

Lastly, there is the basic disanalogy that language is used for communication whereas perceptions are not. This consideration probably will prove final to many, yet I feel that the semantical similarities just mentioned and correlated ones that will presently appear justify the application, with caution and as a metaphor, of the phrase "natural language" to our perceptual experience.

In one way my choice of the term "conventional language" may be bad. It suggests a source in some sort of social agreement, and although this is almost always present in what I have in mind, it is not a necessary element, at least not in all its functions, in building a knowledge of fact. But that term quite properly conveys a sense of arbitrariness and of intermediation which is or springs from something which is essential. Conventional language uses signs which are physical things or events in their own right and which need have no inherent connection with what they designate or assert. Their reference is attached externally to them, so to speak, by rule. This is brought strikingly to our attention by the dissimilarity of words for the same thing in everyday languages. "Red" and "rouge" are sufficiently different to call attention to the fact that they have no likeness to the color they both mark out. As just mentioned, social agreement is not absolutely necessary to the phenomena I have in mind. One may have a private language of one's own, consisting perhaps of no more than certain muscular sets or postural attitudes, but it is still conventional in my sense if these signs are physical occurrences perceivable in their own right and related to what they mean only by externally imposed regularities. Our natural language of sensory impressions is not like this; its symbols are, in a way, the very entities symbolized, yet also, in a way, not. I shall try to explain this enigmatic statement in a moment.

But now that we have this sharp distinction it is necessary to admit that in everyday situations we frequently have mixtures and cases that are difficult to classify. I remember witnessing a floating pile-driver capsize in the harbor of our yacht club and, while seeing a man scrambling down the scaffolding, suddenly hearing myself exclaim, "Why, it's Ivan Thorp and he can't swim!" Now it would be easy enough to separate this into two parts, one in the natural language of perception, the other in conventional English, and this could be justified. But such a procedure is not wholly fair to the situation. My perceptual identification of the man was in part effected by my uttering his name; the latter was not just a translation of a recognition of him that had already occurred. Indeed, most of us talk to ourselves most of the time, so that pure perceptions, perceptions devoid of all conventional expressions, are very rare.

Conventional symbols acquire their meaning; natural symbols are meaningful at birth. The former have their meaning conferred upon them by rule. I shall not here enter upon an investigation of rules in general or of semantical rules in particular. Suffice it to say that although a rule is capable of making a mark or a sound meaningful, and of creating just the meaning that such an entity shall have (within the conventional language in which it is a rule), it cannot create the nature or, if you please, the essence of meaning or referring. Take an analogy. Navigators can by rule require that the port running light on boats shall be red; they do not by any legislation create the distinction between port and starboard. So English can, by its conventions, make "red" refer to a certain color, but it no more creates the nature of designation than it does the color designated. For this, conventional language must look elsewhere; this other place is natural language, that is, perceptions.

We may seem to be faced with an initial problem before we can analyze reference in its primordial form. How are we to get at "natural language"? The problem is really double, in each case involving us in an entanglement with conventional speech. First, our method has committed us to reliance on the language of everyday, that is, conventional language. This is somewhat qualified by the admission that ordinary experience is shaped by and itself shapes, to an unascertainable extent, the grammar of conventional talk. But still something of a difficulty is left, so that we must get at the native tongue of perception in some degree through the conventions we are trying to pass beyond. Second, whatever our success in this, we must formulate it, for communication to others, in conventional words. There is, I think, no general and definitive solution to these problems; we must do the best we can with conventional tools; actually, however, it may turn out better than these abstract forebodings might suggest. So, then, to our problem of meaning in its original state.

We do not, in ordinary sensory perception, experience properties *per se*; we experience them as properties of things or events. "I saw red" is an improper expression, save as a metaphor for "I was suddenly enraged." "I saw a red flag," "I saw a red sunset" or even "I saw something red" are quite all right. Moreover, these things or events we experience as propertied in various ways are external, objective to our perceptions themselves. We can ask what color someone saw the book or dress to be, but not what color the seeing or perceiving was. This is common speech, but now it is well to introduce some jargon, which will be minimal and relatively unobjectionable. Let us speak of properties "as exemplified" and "as experienced." The red of the sunset is the red "as exemplified" by that event. The red to be found in our perception is not, taken in that context, exemplified but experienced; specifically, it is experienced as exemplified by something else, namely, the sunset. We do not speak of the perception as red, for to do so would be to attribute to it red "as exemplified." Still, in it, red is experienced; and this is genuine, honest red, not the three-letter word, "red," nor a monosyllabic vocable.

So here we have the basis of designation, designation as it occurs originally, prior to conventional rules. In our example, the red as experienced names, designates, means, immediately the red as exemplified; the red of the perception refers to the red of the sunset. Not that there are two reds here (supposing the perception veridical), but the red in one capacity or status means the red in the other.

All of the sensory qualities and most of the spatio-temporal relations in our perceptions are there as experienced. Some of the latter, however, are present in the other sense, that is, as exemplified by the perceptions. All perceptions have temporal properties; it is always admissible to ask, "When did you see him?", "At what time did you first notice the dripping sound?" and so on. There has been some prejudice traditionally against admitting that perceptual experiences exemplify spatial as well as temporal relations, but our criterion of common speech is unequivocal. "Where did you first hear the knocking in your motor?," answer, "Going up Stroud Hill", and "At what location did you see the aurora borealis?," answer, "At Ellison Bay, Wisconsin," are entirely acceptable questions and replies.

It may be quite correctly pointed out that we seldom if ever speak of the spatial location of our perceptions *simpliciter;* we ordinarily talk about where the person was when he perceived this or that. The same, I would urge, is true of the temporal locations of our perceptual experiences; we ask when someone saw this or heard that. And this is significant. The existential features of perceptions, the properties they exemplify, are attached to them as experiences of people, not as events in their own right.

In this last respect, perceptions may appear quite different from sentences; it is not clear however that they are completely dissimilar. As mounds of ink or sequences of sound, sentences get out in the world on their own. But it is questionable whether such events, simply so taken, are sentences in our sense. In so far as they refer assertively and so are true or false they would seem to require interpretation and understanding, and thus to be tied to people and their experiences. So it may be well to speak of their spatio-temporal properties not as those of the books containing them or the air-waves shaped to them but as those of the experiences people have in understanding them and possibly also in accepting or rejecting them. If this is valid, then we can place conventional sentences along with perceptual experiences, both taken as events, in the subject-matter of psychology. Our concern as epistemologists is not with them in this existential aspect but simply in their character of being about something other than themselves and their reliability in this regard.

The status of a property as experienced is as ultimate and irreducible as its status as exemplified. The failure to recognize this, and the correlated tendency to treat exemplification as the only way properties are present in the world has led to the invention of images, representatives, mental states as subjects of such characterization. Common sense has not accepted this duplication, however. When someone in an everyday situation sees a blue bird he has no temptation to ascribe the blue to anything but the bird, and specifically not to some idea or inner picture in his mind. Still, the property as experienced is more complex than the property as exemplified. The former refers to the latter; whereas the converse is not true. There could be a world of blue birds and red flags without experience of them, in which the only possible status of blues and reds would be as exemplified. There could not be a world of experienced properties without at least the possibility of these properties' being exemplified, for "experienced" is elliptical for "experienced as exemplified." Experience is thus parasitical upon exemplification, not as a separate growth, but as a requirement of its own nature.

Of course we can think of properties not as properties but simply as the characters or qualities they are, say a certain red or blue. But this occurs through the use of conventional signs which allow us to abstract from the *ascription to* something as red or blue which is always present in concrete perception. This power of abstraction is one of the values of conventional language in extending our knowledge beyond direct perception.

4

Conventional Language As a Supplement to Perception

THE PRESENT chapter will attempt to point up the need of supplementing the language of direct perception by conventional language, but also to warn of the dangers in this extension of our basis of factual knowledge.

There are two kinds of sentences in our ordinary conventional language that are very closely related to our perceptions—so closely that I may speak of them as directly verified by what may be called their "perceptual originals." They are easily confused but it is highly important for our enterprise that they not be. One of them describes its original and thereby tacitly, at least, asserts its existence. I shall call it a "perception-depicter." Here are some instances: "First I saw a bright red flash, then I heard a rumble, finally everything was confused," "Just as I noticed him I heard someone call his name." The other puts into conventional language some phase of its original; it is a partial translation of it. I shall name it a "perception-proxy." Examples are: "The pitcher is winding up, there goes the ball, it's a strike," "The explosion has occurred; there is a bright fire-ball mushrooming up into the sky." The object of the perception-depicter is the perception, of the perception-proxy, the perception's object.

In everyday situations these two kinds of sentences are frequently mixed. Take, in its appropriate setting, the following: "There, I see him! He's just stepping into the train. We must stop him." It would seem pedantic to say of this, "There, I see him!" is a perception-depicter, whereas "He's just stepping into the train" is a perception-proxy, for the whole thing is too much of a piece. Moreover, it probably was just an accident that the sentence was formulated as it was. The speaker could no doubt have expressed himself quite as well by, "There he is! He's just stepping into the train. We must stop him." This clearly contains no perception-depicter. For philosophical purposes it is well to keep the two types separate.

The main role played by conventional language in factual inquiry falls to proxies, not to depicters of perceptions. We do of course speak of "reports" of our observations and personal experiences, and this word, taken out of context, might suggest statements about the perceptions in question, but in the vast majority of cases (outside introspective psychological descriptions) the reports are proxies, are about the observed (of course, as it was observed), not the observations (as occurring). For example, a report of an observer describes an atomic explosion in terms of its apparent height, its changing shape, its colors, and so on.

At this point we should remind ourselves of a distinction noted earlier. Our perceptions "have" properties in two different senses. First, in the strict sense, being themselves events, perceptions exemplify their own properties—any actual perception is mine or yours, occurs at a certain time and not another, has frequently specifiable effects upon the person experiencing it. Among these are the properties of asserting just what it does about its object. But what it so asserts (as contrasted with its assertion thereof) is present in it as experienced, not as exemplified. Suppose I see you sneeze. The sneezing is *yours,* and I so see it. *Your* nose twitches, *your* hand plunges in your pocket for a tissue, *you* make an explosive noise. These properties are in *my* perception but only as asserted of *you*. The properties actually exemplified by my perception are that it is mine, occurs about the same time as your sneeze, causes some amusement in me (not in you—I observe that you are embarrassed, not amused), and so on. Most important, my perception is about you, while your sneeze is not about me, you or anything.

Now, depicters of perceptions describe their objects, namely perceptions, in terms of properties they are taken strictly to "have," properties claimed to be existentially present in them. Proxies describe not the perceptions for which they substitute but the objects of the latter. They assert the properties present in their perceptual originals as experienced, properties these perceptions do not exemplify but only assert. I revert to this distinction because of its importance. If we drop it we are on the way to phenomenalism and solipsism, to the view that all factual knowledge is, in the last analysis, about perceptions or experience only and never about physical things—indeed that it is only about my own personal experience, for it appears undeniable that perceptions are private, and thus that yours are just as external to me as are clouds and mountains.

Moreover, if we try to make depicters of perceptions the basic elements of our knowledge of fact in the region of conventional language, we get all mixed up with judgments extraneous to the perceptual originals which are to serve as our ultimate ground. If I say, "He perceived that the door was ajar," I import on unspecified grounds the assumption that the door was ajar; contrariwise, if I say, "He imagined that the door was ajar," I bring in my judgment that the door was not ajar. If I say, "He thought he saw that the door was ajar," I introduce an element of doubt into his mind that may not have been there at all. Hence, it is better on the whole, and when the perceptual originals are not in conflict or open to special suspicion, to have them represented in conventional language by their direct substitutes.

This does not mean that these proxies can in their own right be used as foundation-stones in our knowledge of fact, for then just saying something is so would make it so and our empirical edifice would crumble. The relationship between perceptual originals and their conventional translations is complex and I can only hope that my suggestion of a simplified model will not be too unfair to what actually occurs in science and everyday life.

It is probably uncontroversial that all our perceptions are, to use the jargon of logic, "singular," that is, have individual things or events as their objects. This does not mean that we cannot perceive several things at once. In fact, we do so in two different ways. On the one hand, we can at one time perceive a number of things individually, as when I see on my untidy desk a knife, a pencil, a pen, a box, a book. I shall take care of this, I hope not too arbitrarily, by saying that a person may have several perceptions at once, some of which, incidentally, may be of parts, external and internal, of his own body. On the other hand, we often do observe groups in their own right as our wealth of words for them discloses—a swarm of bees, a herd of cattle, a fleet of boats. In these cases we experience the members of the group not merely individually but as parts of a whole which is itself apprehended as an individual. We never perceive a class simply as a class (in the logical sense of this term), that is, whatever, but only whatever, satisfies some definition, whether descriptive (*per genus et differentia*) or by enumeration. In the case of a "group," as I have called it, there is always also present an added and directly perceivable bond: usually it is spatial, as in the examples just given, but it might be temporal, as in the nurse's observation of the resumed regularity of the patient's breathing, the audience's recognition of the dot-dot-dot-dash rhythm in Beethoven's Fifth Symphony or the reader's sense of the sonority of the iambic pentameter of Milton's Paradise Lost. We do sometimes speak of "seeing a general principle" or "perceiving an empirical law," but these expressions seem quite clearly to be metaphorical.

This singularity of the propositions of our natural language is a serious defect in so far as we want generalized knowledge of fact, whether for scientific or merely practical purposes. But even for our knowledge of individual facts, pure perceptions reveal deficiencies upon inspection. They contain neither demonstratives nor proper names. This is perhaps partly just a verbal specification. When I meet with perceptions containing demonstratives or proper names I refuse to call them "pure." But it is in part observational, also. I find that I have perceptions which are descriptive or predicative throughout and are in fact quite devoid of conventional symbols. (No perception is pure in the sense of being free of all influence of everyday categories.)

Now, our conventional proxies for perceptions, by furnishing symbols of the kinds mentioned, give us great help in making definite our reference to the individuals about which or whom we are making predications. In pure perceptual experience we have batteries of predications, so to speak. These are "of" individuals; any one individual is selected in perception for predication simply by the whole battery of predications made of it, the "it" being that which is asserted by the perception to exemplify them all together with an indefinite number of unspecified other properties from which the perception has selected just the ones whose assertion constitutes that perception. Our conventional proxies break up and simplify this method of selecting the individual. In ordinary English, we have a subject and predicate, or subject, transitive verb, object (which Russell has shown can be treated as a predicate with two subjects taken in a definite order). The subject or subjects in a singular perception-proxy are particles (such as demonstratives), proper names or definite descriptions (which latter on analysis are seen to involve generalization and so must be set aside for the present).

For example, as I write this I have a perception of something about six inches long, hexagonal in cross-section, hard, for the most part yellow, held between my fingers, one end, which is pointed, being pushed along the paper before me, and so on. It is a great simplification to translate this by the proxy, "This is yellow" or "This pencil is yellow," or even "I hold a yellow pencil." The demonstrative or personal pronoun here serves to pick out the individual (or one of the individuals) about which a single predication is made. This is not a falsification of the original perception, but it is a decided simplification. As such, it is valuable—it readies the perception for generalization; it puts it in such a form that if its truth is in doubt the specific predication questioned is pulled out of the totality forming the perception; it makes any difficulties about identification of the subject or subjects more readily specifiable, and otherwise makes the perception it translates more manageable for further cognitive manipulation. But this simplification is not itself, strictly, an element in our empirical basis; it can serve in this capacity only in so far as it is an acceptable substitute for or translation of a perceptual original.

But now I would be misunderstood if I were to leave the impression that this introduction of particles and proper names in conventional proxies and the simplification of predication they permit are without any basis in their perceptual originals. Consider some analogues. Most English demonstratives retain a modicum of descriptive significance so that some analogue of them can be found in wholly predicative perception. The adverbs "here," "there," the demonstrative adjectives "this" one, "that" one (whatever "one" may designate), as well as the demonstrative pronouns ("this," "that," used absolutely) all clearly have spatial connotation. And this is not to be denied on the score that it is relative to the position of the speaker. "To the right of," "above," "farther away than" are just as relative, yet no one would deny that they are predicative. Even personal pronouns have some descriptive significance, "I" indicating the speaker, "you" the one addressed and so on.

Every perception predicates several properties at once to its object. When I see a chair I experience it as brown, with highlights and shadows, in such and such shapes, and (by association) as hard, smooth and cool. Although I have no way of getting at it perceptually save through properties I experience it as having, still it is not these properties. My experience is of the properties as exemplified, not of them as a class of entities in their own right. This already furnishes a grip for proper names. But practically we are limited in the number of proper names at our disposal. Fortunately experience comes to our aid. I refer to the sense of recognition of an individual we frequently have in perception. It requires but is not reducible to the repetition of a significant group of predications about a single individual. The further thing needed, I believe, is the feeling that in the group of re-experienced properties there are some that are in some fashion peculiar, that serve to mark out the individual perceived from others of its kind.

All this is put not only too definitely but also in a misleading way. I have stated it as though we already had the mechanisms of generalization in pure perception (by using the expression, "others of its kind") and as though properties could be objects of predication at this level (by speaking of some of them as "peculiar"). But bear in mind that I am forced to use conventional language about perception to point out certain features of it. I think it is undeniable that, however we describe it, we do at the primary level of sensory perception "recognize," sometimes correctly, sometimes erroneously, an individual we have experienced before and we do so without the use of a proper name.

As has been indicated, the major defect of pure perceptions is that they contain no mechanisms of generalization. It is in furnishing these that conventional language makes its greatest contribution to our knowledge of fact. Here again the addition is not completely baseless. To simplify matters let us follow traditional Western logic and concern ourselves with two only, after the model of Aristotle. They are expressed in the "particular" and the "universal" propositions. Both presuppose the notion of a class. The former predicates about some member or members of a class, the latter about all. And they do so, as Aristotle would say, "as such"—that is, their reference to the individuals being described is precisely by these devices (of speaking of "some" or of "all" of a specified class or by using equivalent expressions).

The idea of a class can take root in the perception of a group. In the members of a group we have a plurality of subjects of similar predication—the birds in a flock or the fish in a school. These subjects must be taken out of the restrictions, particularly spatio-temporal, involved in being an object of perception, and this can be done through conventional signs such as "bird" or "fish." Besides this, of course, we need devices for *some* and *all*.

The analogue of the first in natural language is any perception of any individual whatever when there is lacking a sense of recognition and thus of the peculiar firmness together of just those predicates by which that individual is recognized. The individual can be thought of (in later, conventional speech) as picked out by any one of the set of predications constituting the perception of it and thus as an instance of that sort of thing; its other predications then become candidates for the predicative function in any conventional proxy for it.

This perhaps calls for a clarification. The particular proposition is often formulated "Some *a*'s are *b*'s," as in the example, "Some streetcars are relics." This is frequently read as equivalent to "A few *a*'s are *b*'s." Now, of course in everyday speech we sometimes do wish to talk indefinitely of a few, but hardly more often than of many or of a more specific proportion of a class—about half, some two-thirds or so forth. The important element for generalization in the particular proposition is its indefiniteness of reference. This is most striking and indeed most useful when an individual is designated simply as a member of the class in question, yet is supposedly identifiable as the subject of several predications, as in "Someone was here and left his umbrella" or "There was some hen that laid this egg."

Recent logic has stressed the existential import of the particular proposition in contrast with the universal. It has treated "Someone has been smoking here" and, in fact, "Some smokers are careless" as asserting that there exists (or has existed) at least one smoker; whereas "All smokers are subject to ejection" and even "Every smoker runs the

risk of developing cancer of the lungs" as making no comparable claim. Is there anything parallel to this in perception? I think not—not because there is no existential affirmation in our perceptual experience but because it per-
meates all of it, is involved in its intentional character, so
that there is nothing corresponding to the symbolic logician's universal proposition which is true by virtue of the
emptiness of its subject class (try to think of the perception-
proxy, "All pencils now before me hover unsupported in
the air" as true because there is no pencil now before me).
Moreover, for the same reason there is no analogue in
perception of a primarily existential assertion, when the
subject is, so to speak, not characterized at all, but occurs,
in the jargon of the logician, as "a variable bound by the
existential quantifier," as in "There is an x such that x is
yellow" or, in better English, "There is something yellow."
Both of these extraordinary cases arise because the logician
wishes to make use of the concept of the null class. I
would not deny him this calculational device, but I doubt
we can make it fit the character of our perceptual experience which, as I have said, always affirms that there is
something that exemplifies the multiplicity of its groups of
predicated properties, though any such assertion may be
false.

The analogue of "all" in natural language is the perception of any group in its aspect of a totality. Psychologically, we perhaps come to the concept through exceptions, by
seeing that "that is not all," as when the child hasn't picked
up all its blocks, and it sees one that has been separated
from the group. But we are not concerned here with psychology. In seeing how and to what degree our conventional "all" translates something in perceptual experience,
we have done the best we can, I think, when we have found
its original in the totality of similar individuals perceived

as forming a group. As already remarked, this is not enough; the "all" is more abstract, for a group is not a logical class, and the "all" of such a class is less concrete than the totality of a spatially and temporally unified group. What needs to be destroyed in going from a group-totality to the concept of every member of a class is the special bond that unites the similar parts into a whole for perception—the herd, the flock, one's pulse, eight bells on the ship's clock. The totality has to shift from this perceivable bond to a merely conceivable completeness of reference to appropriately similar individuals—to all cattle, all geese, every heartbeat, each stroke of the bell.

It is important to avoid a misinterpretation. I do not mean to assert that the analogues in perception to these conventional supplements—the subject-predicate form, demonstratives, proper names, particular and universal generalizations—when they occur justify in any strict sense the use of the latter in their proxies. Any translation is a risky undertaking, and this is especially so in the type of case before us in which changes are instituted to aid in the knowledge-process. In particular, any generalization must satisfy the canons of inductive logic. On this problem I have nothing to say in the present context. What I have tried to do is, rather, to show that these additions to our primary experience can have meaning in terms of that experience and are consequently not left floating in the air of sheer convention. Clearly the way of the logical atomist is closed to any commonsensical empiricist. That way led to the complete destruction of factual significance of "all," "some," "not"—such conventional signs were merely logical devices, "operators," "connectives," which could be dispensed with in our factual knowledge with no greater loss than a bit of time and energy on our part. But if, for example, we had no sense whatever of what, in terms of perception, we could mean by saying that all crows are black, we would be in a bad way indeed in our knowledge, and especially our scientific knowledge, of fact.

But now we come to a conventional modification of our natural language which seems to require strict justification and yet definitely appears to involve an increment. I refer to the use of the negative, although to all appearances our perceptual experience is positive throughout. I feel quite assured of the meaningfulness and even the truth of the proposition that there is no lizard on the desk before me at the present moment, yet how can I see any such thing? Whatever I perceive I perceive as positively present in the world.

There are philosophers who say that negatives, although convenient, are not strictly necessary for our knowledge so long as we have the mechanisms of generalization. They would say that the sentence "No lizard is on the desk before me" can be properly restated as "Everything in the universe is other than a lizard on the desk before me." In some obvious sense this last sentence does omit any symbol of negation. But what is meant by "other than"? I personally cannot understand it in this context in any other way than as denying identity, but this would reintroduce a negation (and in fact multiply its attachment enormously— from the lizards on the desk before me to everything in the universe). And similar remarks can be made about other generalizations suggested as devices that can take the place of the negative. Let me mention one more: "Every lizard is elsewhere than on the desk before me." What, in this sentence, does "elsewhere than" mean? It seems to me that it is used to deny identity, the identity of each place occupied by a lizard with any place on the desk.

Now, the reason it seems necessary to justify at least some negatives is that they are used in singular propositions where one is apparently risking no generalization upon perception but is simply recasting it. Consider such cases as "Richard is not here," "The pencil is not round," "The thermometer does not register 0° C." The problem of the verification of such statements as these cannot be handed over to science or inductive logic because sentences of this kind purport to be direct renditions in conventional language of perceptual experiences: the difficulty caused by the fact that those experiences are positive throughout cannot be delegated to any one else; we philosophers must deal with it ourselves.

The first step in solving our problem is relatively easy. We simply note that if these proxies are faithful to their originals, the latter must omit the predications involved, for example, must omit any combination of properties by which we recognize Richard. But this is clearly not sufficient to warrant translations of them by negatives. The kind of intentionalism we are developing allows many omissions which cannot be treated as denials, for it is selective. A true perception contains, as experienced or as asserted of its object, only a few of the latter's properties, and we must not say that it denies all those which it does not assert. For example, I see the thermometer but do not touch it; my perception therefore omits tactile properties. But this does not permit me to report, via conventional language, "The thermometer is not hard." Suppose I see the pencil from one side only, and this perception of it omits all printing on it. This does not allow me to say, "The pencil has no printing on it," although it does justify, "The pencil has no printing on its near side."

What more, then, do we need to warrant translating an omission of predications in our perception by a denial of them in our proxy? We need the presence of conflicting or incompatible predications, which is the second step in our solution. It, too, may seem relatively simple at first. Many properties form classes that have this characteristic of incompatibility. Colors do, and also tactile qualities and shapes and locations. If the spot on the tablecloth is red it cannot also be green; the pencil's being hexagonal prohibits its being round; when the top of the mercury column is at the place marked "10° C" it cannot also be at the location labeled "0° C."

But now our troubles really begin. Taste qualities, for example, and pitches, similarly, fail to form such incompatible classes, as bittersweet chocolate and the noise of a trolley or a resonant tone of a bass singer attest. And if Einstein is correct, a motion that is slower than another may also be faster than it, an event before another may be after it as well.

This is bad enough in itself, but what is worse, questions are raised about the other cases, the cases in which different predications do conflict. The fundamental one is, what is the basis of this incompatibility in instances in which it does occur? The only answer that fits our empirical point of view is that its foundation is experience, for it surely is a matter of fact and not of logic. I hope it is clear that I am speaking not of the genesis but of the grounds of this distinction. But if the grounding is experience, then we face a paradox. We have been trying to find at our empirical basis, namely in pure perceptions themselves, that which will warrant the use of negatives. We seemed to discover what we were looking for in omissions of predications when these are accompanied by the presence of incompatible ones. But now we are forced to admit that this incompatibility is empirically based. This seems to be an obvious circle. It can be put in another way. If we say that colors are incompatible but pitches not, locations are incompatible but velocities not, we are indulging in generalizations.   Now, generalizations are not to be found in our natural language; they require conventional mechanisms as we have seen.   But the phenomenon of incompatibility we wanted in order to justify singular, negative proxies was at the perceptual level.

To talk about incompatibilities and even omissions of predication requires the use of conventional language and of its devices of generalization.   But these devices are frequently justified; they are, I think, in the case before us. Perceptions cannot speak of what they omit, or of the conflict of some of the omitted predications with some of those present.   But *we* can with conventional sentences.   Thus we can say of perceptions that quite generally the presence of an asserted color is accompanied by the omission of other color-predications ascribed to exactly the same individual thing, but we cannot (since it is not true) say the comparable thing about pitches and individual noises.

This means not only that we cannot admit that perceptions ever strictly deny anything (which is something we have maintained from the first), but also that no one perception ever strictly justifies a negative proxy for it; the justification is by the original as supplemented by generalizations that appropriately apply to it.

This leads me to call the negative we have been discussing "empirical."   We run a risk arising from the tacit generalization involved whenever we translate a perception by the use of a negative.   Indeed, judging by my own experiences, color predications are not always incompatible (I have seen surfaces that were two colors at once, for example, a yellow pencil observed through blue glasses), whereas we often treat tastes as though they were mutually exclusive, although often also as though they were not. However, this is a peril we must frequently assume; we cannot carry on the enterprise of acquiring knowledge of fact without the use of the empirical negative.

Perhaps I can make my point about the character of this "empirical negative" by revising an old tale. When Eve emerged from Adam's rib, her first perception was that of a green apple. She did not perceive it to be red, but neither did she see it to be not red. It was just green (and of course round and shiny and altogether delectable). Now Adam was a dull fellow, leading a purely vegetative life with no perception of anything at all. Yet it was necessary to be attractive to him (who else was available?). So Eve invented language, and her first word was "no."

As time went on Eve had other perceptions. She saw a red rose. And she increased her vocabulary to include "rose," "red," "apple" and "green." Adam being such a dunce, she found herself playing with her own ideas. "Apple red?" she said, with rising inflection. "No," was her response.

Now the Creator, who beheld all her thoughts, was disturbed. "That little minx is too inquisitive; I shall have to expel her from the Garden and occupy her with work," He thought. Yet He was, despite Himself, intrigued. "Is she," He wondered, "justified in saying, 'No'? What, in terms of her perceptions, does it mean? Clearly only that she does not perceive the apple to be red, not that she sees that it is not-red but rather green, for note, she says nothing about its being green; moreover she hasn't the experience to generalize to the truth (even if she had the verbal mechanisms to do it, which, clever as she is, she will soon devise) that green things are never also red. At this stage, green and red are to her like green and round—the apple can be both at once. She hasn't seen anything green and red but she might, at any moment, for all she knows—the world is young."

Weeks pass. The Great Sin is committed. Eve has let her curiousity wander from her knowledge of fact to that of value, and as a result she, with her poor dumb mate, has had to give up the ease of the Garden for the toil of the Desert. But she is still inquisitive, and she thinks back about her traumatic experience. "The apple was red when I tasted it. Was it still also green? No. How could it be if it was red? Nothing red is also green. I'm a woman of experience now, no longer a naïve girl. And I've never seen anything red to be green. Yet . . . yet . . . ," and here she catches her breath, "it did taste both sweet and sour!"

The need for supplementing perceptions by conventional language as the ground of factual knowledge rests largely on our demand for generalization and the readying of singular propositions to serve as bases for this process. So far, we have been concerned mainly with the mechanisms of generalization and how they can have a meaning in perceptual terms when all our perceptions are singular. We must now consider a related but somewhat less important supplement to perceptual experience. That experience, strictly, consists, in each case, of one's own perceptions of the moment plus what one can directly remember, that is, remember without the aid of conventional symbols. This supplement is too narrow in content for any significant generalization: confined to it we could verify no important scientific laws nor even any practical rules to guide conduct. We need to make available larger resources. Our ideal aim of course would be to make all perceptions that actually occur accessible. In practice, this goal cannot be achieved but we must do whatever we reasonably can towards its attainment.

Conventional speech makes social communication possible. Perhaps the necessity of "convention" is not immediately appreciated, so let me remind you that, as I use the term, gestures, facial expressions and other forms of bodily behavior, not usually classified as speech, are instances of conventional language since they utilize physical events other than their objects of reference to designate or affirm the latter.

Now the social use of language serves many purposes, as our linguistic analysts never tire of pointing out, but this truth cannot be employed to deny the equally valid contention which we are making, namely, that social communication makes available for our knowledge of fact vast resources of perceptual experience that would otherwise be closed. Without reports from other observers concerning what they have directly perceived, any given scientist would find himself intolerably confined. And these reports, in the last analysis, take the form of perception-proxies.

Moreover, these conventional substitutes for direct perceptions also help to make available an investigator's own past perceptions, thereby extending, so to speak, the field of his accurate memory. He writes down what he observes, so that he can tabulate it, summarize it, apply statistical methods to it. Indeed, even before writing it down he usually has introduced conventional symbols (such as numerals and other devices on his instruments) and occasionally trusts his memory not of the exact, total original perceptions, but of such simplified proxies into which he had translated them for his purposes.

All this I think is beyond controversy and quite elementary, once one has agreed to use the categories with which we are operating. I shall therefore not elaborate the obvious except to say that in many, many other ways conventional speech is vital to any living pursuit of factual knowledge. This, however, makes all the more imperative our notice of the dangers involved.

The use of proxies introduces several types of possible error not present if we were to limit ourselves to pure perceptions. I shall mention four as typical and important.

(1) By importing conventional symbols in the form of physical things or events which must be apprehended in their own right, proxies open an added possibility of misperception not present in our natural language. Suppose, looking at a Van Gogh, you say, "His sunflowers literally glow in the sunshine," whereas, I mistake you to say, "His sunflowers literally grow in the sunshine," we would then have an instance of this type of error, which is a misapprehension of a conventional sign in its properties as a physical thing.

(2) Considered as physical entities, as mere sounds or visual patterns, conventional signs are not symbolic. To become so, they need to be employed in the intentional processes of minds, which, to serve the purposes of perception-proxies, must involve arbitrary rules and indeed, for communication, socially accepted ones. These rules may be unknown or misapplied in particular cases. An instance from personal experience may be amusing. I saw in a recent issue of the *Japan Times* a picture of a number of diplomats all facing the reader. One of them was a foreign functionary who was identified in the accompanying description as the man on Prime Minister Kishi's left. This led me entirely astray until I learned that "on so-and-so's left" is not used by Japanese to mean to one's left when one assumes so-and-so's orientation, as it is by Americans, but to the left of so-and-so from the standpoint of the one addressed, in this case the reader of the newspaper. In this case there was no misperception of the physical signs; the mistake turned on a misunderstanding of the rules converting them from things into linguistic symbols.

The kind of risk we run here is open to empirical safeguards; it is a matter of actual rules of actually employed languages and appears always as an individual problem in individual cases.   It is well to note that we are not faced with a systematic problem that might be thought to be involved in the position we are developing.

For a sound or pattern of ink-marks to function as a symbol it must get ensnared in linguistic rules.   But this is nothing that happens to it directly or physically; as a physical thing it is not modified by this adventure, adding a trill if it be a sound or an arrow if an ink-mark.   The rule simply directs us to attach a meaning, not literally to the external entity, but to our perceptions of it.   The countless millions of printed characters buried in the stacks of our scholarly libraries, touched by no living being save perhaps an occasional, undiscriminating bookworm, are no more symbols than are the shelves upon which the tomes repose or the dust that has settled upon these caskets through the ages.   To come semantically to life they must be seen and thus enter our native tongue of perception.

This may be stated in a paradoxical form that seems to involve us in a vicious circle: proxies for our perceptions must themselves occur as perceptions; our conventional language is just a part of our natural language.   The paradox is eased, however, when we note that all we need here is to have natural sentences play a double role: as quite ordinary perceptions of physical entities and as perceptions to which, by virtue of their having just those entities as their objects which they do have, we attach some arbitrary rule of meaning.   They thus refer twice over: on the one hand, without benefit of rules, to the vocal utterances or black marks we loosely speak of as conventional symbols but are now considering as physical events, on the other, through rules, to the things conventionally designated by these entities, now considered as symbolic.

We must avoid like the plague the mistake of supposing that perceptions in this dual semantical role are, in the terms of recent logic, in a "meta-language," or, put in the scholastic phrase, "of second intention." They are not perceptions of perceptions, sentences about sentences. As perceptions their objects are simply and directly physical things; by the rules which convert them into proxies, their objects are the objects of their perceptual originals—again, although this time indirectly or conventionally, physical things. For example, you hear someone say, "The sun is shining" and you understand what he means. In this experience you hear the sounds: the object of this perception is simply that sequence of noises. By convention, however, the noises function as a substitute for or partial translation of a perception of the sun's shining—as such, their object is neither that perception nor any statement about the sun nor reference to it, but the sun's shining, itself. Unclarity at this point would confound everything we have been doing; clarity, however, resolves the apparent paradox of circularity mentioned a short while ago.

(3) Even in cases in which we neither misperceive the proxy nor misapprehend, through a misapplication of linguistic rules, the meaning it is intended to convey, we may still fall into error due to the fact that it may mistranslate the perceptual original for which it is a substitute. All translation modifies meaning somewhat; specifically in this case, the proxy always impoverishes its perceptual original. Think of the most commonplace perception, say of a fly crawling along the back of your hand—how much is omitted of its detail by the proxy you utter: "There is a fly crawling along the back of my hand"! This would be true no matter how extensive our vocabulary; add to it then the fact that even the most expert of us in any given field of observation find our available words insufficient for our

powers of discrimination. Painters themselves do not have separate names for every discriminable color nor wine-tasters for every nuance of taste and aroma—how much poorer are most of us in our linguistic resources! This omissiveness and inarticulateness common to the best of our conventional substitutes for perception does not of it-self constitute error, but it is an ever-present source of possible mistake. From the lack of color-names we may be led to suppose that two pigments have the same hue when they do not; from the omissiveness of our conventional statement, we may suppose a liquid to be colorless when it may have an observable and actually observed, but not reported, color.

Besides these universal deficiencies in all translation of our perceptions into conventional language there are many specific defects in various particular vernaculars, ambigui-ties of words and syntax and other faults too numerous to list. It is in fact amazing that we get on as well as we do in putting perceptual experience into ordinary language.

(4) We must not ignore, though these perhaps are least important, the cases of sheer misrepresentation, when a sentence presented as a proxy for some experience has no perceptual original at all or one flatly incompatible with what is stated in the conventional substitute for it. These range all the way from downright lying through pathologi-cal self-deception to mild manipulation of the truth for dramatic or humorous purposes.

I do not present the foregoing classification of errors which can occur when translating perceptions into their conventional proxies as exhaustive: heaven knows that lan-guage is too lively for any such imprisonment; but it may serve as a sort of warning of the dangers we assume in mak-ing available in a suitable form for our knowledge of fact as much of our stock of pure perceptions as possible.

Any particular proxy should stand ready at all times to have its credentials challenged—is it a proper substitute for its original, never of course in all respects but always in those in which it purports to be an equivalent as regards the specific service to be rendered in the extension or verification of our knowledge of fact?

Frequently when a perception-proxy is challenged it is as a statement of fact, not as a rendition into conventional terms of a perceptual original. Thus if I assert, "You have my billfold in your hand," and you deny it, you probably mean to deny that you hold my billfold, not that I have put into correct conventional language what I directly perceive. This kind of disagreement will be investigated later. Sometimes, however, we are concerned with the type of error which has been discussed in this lecture. Suppose a patient tells a psychiatrist, "There is a devil coming to get me," and the psychiatrist replies, "You are malingering; you have no such hallucination at all"; or an expert winetaster tells a novice, "You are mistaken; the wine does taste bitter but it is also sweet; you must pay closer attention to your experience." We would then have cases of suspicion that proxies are, at least in part, improper renditions of perceptual experience.

When this occurs the challenge and any reply to it are usually formulated as (in our terminology) "perception-depicters," that is, as descriptions in conventional language of perceptions. Any conflict here would appear not in the form of rival statements about the object of perception but of competing descriptions of some perception of it, if, for example, the dispute turned not on whether there was a devil coming to get the patient but on whether the patient was having such an experience. Such perception-depicters perform a perfectly legitimate role in our pursuance of factual knowledge.

There is also another part that perception-depicters take, a more positive one, in the increase of our knowledge of fact. We often want to know about the occurrence of perceptions themselves: this is a matter of fact and one subject, though with many difficulties and hazards, to empirical investigation. I do not propose to explore this thorny field at present. But I do want to point up once more a danger. Although depicters of our perceptions do perform these functions, as well as another to be mentioned when we consider the reliability of perceptions in their own right, and thus must be placed with proxies for perceptions as supplementing pure perceptions in giving a basis for our knowledge of fact, we must not confuse them with proxies nor allow them to replace the latter, as though perceptions and perception-depicters were sufficient to ground our factual knowledge. Such an elimination of proxies would almost inevitably lead to some form of subjectivism.

Strictly, phenomenalism, and its natural though not logical consequence, solipsism, are ontological positions claiming that only sensory experience, and, in the latter case, specifically my experience, exists. But one is led into these positions by epistemological considerations, by the assumption that I can have as objects of my belief and thus of my knowledge only my own experience. All of this is very much out of harmony with our everyday ways of speaking and thinking.

One way sometimes taken to try to bring such positions into some semblance of harmony with the latter is by constructing not only physical things, but the experiences of others as well, out of sets of my perceptions. I think this amounts to a subterfuge. Consider the second of these constructions; you see something, let us say, that I do not—an insect or an airplane. Suppose you tell me about it. On the phenomenalist's account you are not speaking about the insect or airplane, but only about your experiences; in the solipsist's story, your visual perceptions become my auditory experiences of "your" reports of them. This is clearly not what we mean, in common speech, by your perceptions. Nor do we use your reports in building our knowledge in a way that fits this pattern. We may investigate whether you said that you saw the insect or airplane, but if we are content with the evidence that you did so report, we do not take this as full and complete evidence that you saw what you said you did; it is at least conceivable that you asserted you saw the airplane when you did not, but if your seeing it just is my hearing you say that you saw it, this would be impossible.

Now we must admit that if we take the position that all perceptions are private, we are faced with a problem: when is one to trust the proxies of other people? But I think this is not a systematic, philosophical dilemma but only an empirical question to be answered anew in each particular case. In a general sense this whole matter of the privacy of our perceptions is an observational issue.

Most of us do not believe that mental telepathy occurs, but it may, and if it does not, this is a fact about our make-up which might have been different. Although I never do feel the pains in your teeth or toes or see things from just the angle of your eyes, the Creator could have made me with this confusing constitution, as apparently, in part, He has Siamese twins, perhaps with just the purpose of keeping me straight on this as being an empirical matter.

And as I have said, in individual cases the reliability of proxies uttered by other people is something to be investigated empirically in just those cases. I have instances of various sorts of errors in translating my own perceptions into appropriate proxies. I watch out for signs of these, similar to those I realize are open to the observation of others in my own case—signs of dishonesty, of inadequate discrimination, of overhasty denial, of misapplication of conventional terms, and so on.

As a consequence, we must admit that we can never be sure when we accept the proxies of others that they are proper equivalents of perceptions that these people experience. But we take a risk in our own case and, indeed, as we shall see, natural language itself can never give us certainty. This is the predicament we are in: all our knowledge of fact rests ultimately on language—partly natural and partly conventional—and language is never beyond suspicion. Only a mystic can claim such complete identity with the object of his knowledge as to escape all possibility of error.

But now if we have avoided solipsism or, more accurately stated, skepticism about the occurrence of any perceptions besides one's own, can we escape another and more basic skepticism—about a world external to all perceptions, others' as well as one's own? Perceptions point outward, so to speak; they are by nature assertions. Perhaps there is nothing outside them to which they point; perhaps there are no physical entities corresponding to their assertions. We shall concern ourselves with this old yet ever new problem in the next chapter.

5

Does Intentionalism Lead
to Skepticism?

DESPITE our leisurely pace, we have been making progress too rapidly. We have extended our whole basis of factual knowledge from occurrent perceptions to their conventional proxies plus even some depicters of them, yet all the while leaving unnoticed the glove thrown down by the ancient skeptic, Sextus Empiricus, and the modern one, René Descartes. "What reason," they ask, "have you to trust perceptions, to say nothing of their conventional substitutes?" And here my odd proposal to call perceptions "sentences" in a "natural" language involves me in added embarrassment. If the whole foundation of our knowledge of fact is linguistic, the house built upon it must be insecure indeed. Have we not got ourselves shut into what may suitably be described by the fearsome phrase, "the linguacentric predicament"? Can we never break out of the circle of words to the things they signify? Must we remain satisfied with (presumably good) intentions? In short, are we not inescapably involved in skepticism?

It is a good policy, whether in a cold war or a hot one, to divide one's enemy. So in our struggle I suggest we separate skepticism into some of its many varieties and see if we cannot come to terms with them one by one.

First, we may be accused of ontological skepticism. In its more extreme form this would say that we have no right to claim the existence of anything beyond our language and what it refers to. If we go back of conventional speech, this would leave us with perceptions as the only things that exist or occur.

Now we might be tempted, as many empiricists have been, to follow the lead of Bishop Berkeley in meeting this challenge. "Let us," he said in substance, "take what is the criterion of existence and make it the thing itself. Let perception be not merely the test of existence but its very essence; then we need not look for some imperceptible primary matter and feel defeated when we discover that we can never get at it."

This escape is closed to us, however, for two basic reasons, one inherent in it and one relative to our intentionalism. G. E. Moore strikingly formulated the first. "To be is to be perceived" won't work because it is circular: it defines existence in terms of the occurrence (that is, the existence) of perceptions. Hypothetical perceptions will not do the trick; only existent ones will.

Relative to our intentionalism Berkeley's "solution" would be disastrous, for it would make all perceptions false —false in principle and beyond all possible correction, for in our view they all assert the existence of external physical events.

But there is no need to follow Berkeley. Simplifying (by ignoring for a moment the complex role of conventional language), we may say that knowledge of physical fact is constituted by perception of it. Thus we are required to admit that the existence of knowledge of this sort is identical with the occurrence of appropriate perception, but not that what is so known is. Quite the opposite: if the objects of this knowledge exist at all they must be different from the occurrence of the knowledge of them. Thus we are still left with the possibility of this "ontological" kind of skepticism; no object of perception may exist, all perceptual experience may be a vast dream.

Now this, though possible and to that extent perhaps embarrassing, is not necessary: our intentionalism does not force us to deny or even seriously to question the existence of an external world. We need at this point do only two things: give up the false goal of Descartes, namely, certainty about matters of fact, and stick to the basis of our whole philosophic approach, to wit, the categories embedded in everyday thought and speech. And the latter is not an empty gesture, as some philosophic layman might think when he notes that all philosophers, with hardly an exception, claim the blessing of common sense for their views. Indeed, even Berkeley himself advanced such a claim, though I think he failed to substantiate it. You remember he had Hylas raise the objection, "But, do you in earnest think the real existence of sensible things consists in their being actually perceived? If so, how comes it that all mankind distinguish between them? Ask the first man you meet, and he shall tell you, *to be perceived* is one thing, and *to exist* is another," to which Berkeley, in the person of Philonous, replied, "I am content, Hylas, to appeal to the common sense of the world for the truth of my notion. Ask the gardener why he thinks yonder cherry-tree exists in the garden, and he shall tell you, because he sees and feels it; in a word, because he perceives it by his senses. Ask him why he thinks an orange-tree not to be there, and he shall tell you, because he does not perceive it."

Berkeley's feeling for the common man is quite sound, hence the subterfuge he uses is only too apparent: he shifts from the everyday idea of what it is for a physical thing to exist (which is not identified with perception of it) to the test or evidence we have of its existence (which is). We will remain true to common sense and keep these two questions distinct.

A less extreme form of ontological skepticism does not deny an external world to which our perceptions refer but does deny or at least question that it is *as* they describe it. This may be divided into two subforms. One, which I shall designate "agnosticism," leaves the whole character of the external world indeterminate, a vast question mark. It may rest its case on the argument that we have no reason for accepting any of the claims made by our perceptions concerning the properties of physical things. This is irrational, however, for what good grounds have we for supposing anything external to exist other than the claim of such existence common to all our perceptions? A better argument points out that frequently we have conflicting perceptual descriptions of the same physical thing or event (from some angles the coin looks round, from others, elliptical); what right have we, then, to play favorites, to take one and put aside its rivals as correctly portraying their common object? Let us, then, put them all aside as regards their concrete descriptions, accepting only their common affirmation that there is something external (so the argument runs).

On this apparently reasonable line of thought I have two comments. First, it does not properly lead to the positive conclusion that external things display none of the properties we perceive them as having. At most, it can only urge upon us a suspension of judgment. Second, this suspension of judgment, taken as final and systematic rather than as a temporary psychological state of mind, does not accord with everyday thought. In ordinary life we do not act and think, when faced with conflicting perceptions, as though they were all equally unworthy of credence. We set aside some as distortions or illusions or dreams precisely because we do not believe they are all equally so classifiable. And we have, I think, fairly definite criteria for separating the more from the less reliable. This is a topic I shall discuss later in connection with a different species of skepticism.

A second and more positive subform of the ontological skepticism now under consideration I shall call "scientism." It agrees that there are physical things that frequently serve as the objects of our perceptions, but it denies that they ever are as we perceive them, claiming rather that they are as "science" describes them, being constituted of fields of force, transformations of energy or minute subatomic particles, completely devoid, of course, of color, odor, taste, sound or any other perceptual quality.

The argument for this position seems strong indeed, but I think it is vulnerable at one point. It says that science, and physical science in particular, has been extraordinarily successful in its predictions, enabling man to control physical events in a remarkable and rapidly increasing degree, whereas common sense and reliance upon what is disclosed in immediate perception have no such achievements to their credit. Therefore we ought to accept the scientific picture of the external world in preference to the commonsensical and directly perceptual one.

We can get at the weakness in this line of thought by asking how we know that physical science has been more successful in making predictions and controlling nature than common sense with its trust in the perceptual description of things. The answer, if you push it to its final form, is that the evidence lies in what is revealed by perceptions— in atomic bombs and submarines, in television and automatic photoelectric doors as seen, heard, felt and otherwise sensibly perceived. This should give us pause. Let us put it differently. Suppose we take away from the physicist all perceptions together with their conventional proxies and depicters. He would then be quite unable to verify his account of external events. Moreover, he would have no language in which to set up his account; his books might have debit and credit columns but by having no way to refer to debtors and creditors they couldn't be audited, they would just be schoolboy exercises or even worse, for such exercises have the semblance of referring. Let him have his "ergs" and "neutrons" and "quanta of energy" but no perceptual or conventional references to cyclotrons, atomic reactors or Wilson cloud chambers, and his "language" would remain unattached, non-designative, that is, no language at all, certainly not a language descriptive of the external world.

Moreover, what can "scientism" do with the predications present in our sensory perceptions—with the colors, odors, warmths we perceive as characterizing physical things? Obviously it must treat all our perceptual descriptions as false (that is why we can classify it as a form of skepticism), but if these properties are not properly predicated of physical things, to what subjects are they to be ascribed? To mental events? But from the inside mental events disown them; they take these qualities not to be properties of themselves but of external things. And from the outside mental events are never observed at all; certainly they are not observed to be colored or odorous or warm or cold. If scientism persists in saying that nevertheless it is mental events that exemplify these properties, then it should admit that it has neither the warrant in general for such a claim nor any methods of verifying it in particular cases.

"Scientism," then, is not too serious a threat to our perceptual intentionalism. It does indicate, however, that we should do something to make our peace with physical science and with the entities with which it, in theory, populates the external world. Let me mention two plausible alternatives. One is taken over from phenomenalism, particularly as developed by Ernst Mach. That view had no place at all for unperceivable entities, such as subatomic particles. It contended, therefore, that these supposed entities should be treated not as realities in the world beyond experience but as useful fictions, as economical intellectual devices by which the physicist can readily organize his generalizations of perceptual occurrences into laws and various patterns of laws. All we need to do to make this alternative available for our own use is to shift the application of these conceptual economies from the occurrences of perceptions to the occurrences of their objects. In general, physical things are as we perceive them, that is, colored, odorous, and so on, but to put their actions and reactions into easily calculable laws, the symbolic fictions of theoretical physics (such as subatomic particles) are brought into play.

This actually fits quite well certain tendencies in recent physics, for example, the growing skepticism of models and the willingness to use different and incompatible patterns of concepts in dealing with different aspects of the same sets of events. But in one respect it seems quite implausible. It is extremely difficult to believe that recent astounding developments in applied physics, based on theories about the tremendous energy bound up within the atom, have arisen from concepts not of realities but of mere fictions, whose sole justification is the economy they have afforded the scientist in dealing with ordinary, sensibly observable matters.

The second alternative for us avoids this implausibility of the first. According to it, the entities of theoretical physics, or in any case some of them, do exist and are as the

physicist describes them.   But it also says that the things
we perceive exist and in some instances have the properties
we perceive them to have, including the so-called sensory
qualities.   It is able to do this by distinguishing whole-
properties from part-properties, and both from what might,
for want of a better name, be called "unbroken properties."

To show what I mean, let us for the moment forget
physics and consider some examples drawn from ordinary
perception.   If we say that the whole of a child's hoop is
green we mean that every segment of it is, and conversely,
if every segment is green, the whole is.   But if we say that
the whole is circular we do not mean that every segment is,
and conversely, to say that every segment is an arc does
not require us to admit that the whole is.   In the first case
we have an unbroken property (green); in the second a
whole-property (circular) and a part-property (having the
form of an arc).   To take another instance, if the whole of
a symphonic movement is in C-minor then every part of it
is and vice versa; but if it has as a whole the structure
a-b-b-a, it does not follow that every part of it does, nor is
the converse true.

Now let us return to our problem.   Our second alternative is able to retain as valid of physical things both
perceptual descriptions of them and accounts rendered in
terms of the properties dealt with in theoretical physics by
saying that when these differ, one from the other, the former
is concerned with whole-properties, the latter with part-
properties.   Now sensory qualities, which are generally
unbroken properties when we are dealing with the objects
of perception, are properly to be considered as whole properties of these objects when they are contrasted with those
described by the theoretical physicist; the physicist is busy
with part-properties.   Thus the child's whole hoop may be
green whereas none of the molecules making it up is.   More-

over we may, if we wish, and personally I do so wish, say that the physicist's part-properties are more effective in explaining the whole-properties of perceived entities than contrariwise, whereas the reverse relation obtains when it comes to verification or factual evidence. Although both atom bombs and subatomic particles exist, on this view, the properties of the latter better explain those of the former than the reverse, whereas those of the former are more easily verified than those of the latter (indeed, in principle furnish all the evidence for the latter).

So much, then, by way of discussion of ontological forms of skepticism. They may be embarrassing to our intentionalism but are not inherently involved in it nor are they natural consequences of it. I turn next to a semantical species that may be thought to be the inescapable outcome of our type of analysis. Perceptions, on our view, have physical things or events as their objects; they consist of assertions about these objects, of predications of properties of them. It is essential to this view that it deny that the objects of perceptions ever get bodily into them. My seeing a grasshopper does not require or permit the grasshopper to hop into my perception of it. Just how, then, can the grasshopper be the object of my perception? If it stays outside must not my perception be an empty, that is, objectless, pointing, a sheer intending without anything specifiable intended?

My first response is quite simple. It is that this supposed skeptical outcome is due to a misconception. In some way the object perceived must be in the perception of it; it must not remain wholly external in the sense of being completely unrelated to the perception. But the relation here is semantical, not existential. The grasshopper is, under this consideration, related to my seeing it simply as its object; this alone is what is demanded by the intention of it; anything further involves some other sort of business between the grasshopper and me. Such further business is no doubt required in order that my perception of the grasshopper actually occur, but it does not form any part of the intention.

But now the objection may be phrased in a more subtle way. If we grant that the object need not enter the perception of it bodily, must it not become part of it in some fashion, or some copy or representative be present? Else how does the perception have just it for its object?

There is point to this and our answer must be carefully formulated. In fact, I think that many intentionalists have gone wrong right here, namely all those who have set up a "content" of perception somehow representing the object but distinct from it as well as from the act of perceiving. For as soon as one does this it is almost impossible to avoid treating this content as the true object of the act of perceiving, and one is on the road to phenomenalism (denying that one ever perceives external things) or skepticism (questioning the relation between the immediate object or content and the ultimate object or external thing).

To avoid this danger I would put aside more recent intentionalism and go back to what seems to me to have been suggested by Aristotle himself, although I may be historically mistaken. The key idea here is the presence in perception of properties simply as experienced, properties which (rightly or wrongly) are taken by the perception to be exemplified by the external thing. Perception simply *is* the predication of these properties, the ascription of them to an object. And this predication is not through some conventional symbols nor even imaginary copies or replicas of them, but by the very properties so predicated, which are abstractly present in the perception, separated, as Aristotle would say, from their matter, that is, from their actual exemplification. Not only is there no other representative of the object, there is likewise no other act of mind. Mind, in the form of perceptual consciousness, *is* just this predication, this selectivity, this presence as more concretely exemplified—that is, exemplified along with other properties —elsewhere, namely in the object.

But do not perceptions occur? Yes, and as such we may if we wish call them "acts," but if we do, it might be better to call them "acts of the body" rather than "acts of the mind." However, even this way of speaking is dangerous, for reasons already noted. Moreover, perceptions are not overt, large-scale acts, like kicking or throwing or biting, but small-scale cerebral ones, neural discharges in the higher centers. And their causes and effects are physiological and not for a moment to be confused with their intentions or the objects of their intentions. We must keep distinct *what* these mental events are, in their character *as mental*, which is intentional or referential, and *that* they are, which is existential. Their properties *as events* are the properties of the neural happenings often said, incorrectly, to be their causes or necessary conditions—such properties as who has them, when and where they are had, how long they last and so on.[1]

My suggestion is that intentions (in the sense of references) are the mental atoms and that they are not events but "aspects," "dimensions," "functions" of physical events, namely, of certain complex neurological events. Intentions are like properties in being incomplete, by nature dependent for existence upon something else, and universal in the sense that the same one may belong to several events. More particularly, they are like relations in holding of or

1. I have tried to state this a little more specifically elsewhere ("The Adequacy of a Neurological Theory of Perception," *Philosophy and Phenomenological Research*, XX [September, 1959], 75-84) and to tie it with my whole commonsensical approach.

between something and something else (a neurological event and a perceived object). But they are unlike properties in that we do not observe them in observing what "has" them. More particularly, they are unlike relations in that they can belong to one of their terms (the neurological event) in the absence of the other (the perceptual object) in cases of error. Finally, they are unlike properties in a certain inherent complexity. They may be said to include ordinary properties, but neither as exemplified by themselves nor by what "has" them but instead by their objects; thus intentions can themselves be called signs, natural or radical signs, identical with their objects (in veridical perception) in the quality or character of those objects' properties but non-identical in the factor of exemplification (in place of exemplification intentions have ascription).

But how, on my suggestion, can we pair intentions correctly with the neurological events that "have" them? Clearly it won't do to say that the brain physiologist just observes two sets of events, namely neural events and intentions, and correlates them by seeing which has which. Still, an indirect empirical procedure is not ruled out. First, people do have certain intentions on certain occasions and fail to have them on others. Second, the brain physiologist can obtain fairly reliable empirical knowledge (although usually demanding some inference through analogy) in some of these cases about the presence or absence of certain neurological patterns of occurrences. That knowledge is sufficient for the tentative pairing which is the best we can accomplish. However, this does require that the physiologist accept reports of his subjects on their experiences and that we (philosophers) admit the meaningfulness of such reports. Such reports can be taken as reports of observations, not of brain events or of mental events (as being themselves occurrences), but of the objects perceived (or hallucinated). Such observations are themselves intentions and their report is evidence of their occurrence.

Finally, it may be feared that our intentionalism may lead to skepticism about verification, to the denial or doubt that we can ever ascertain, with any degree of reliability, which of our conflicting perceptions are true. This furnishes us a more substantial challenge, one which we must answer more fully and concretely. It is based on the fact that intentionalism, as here presented, requires a correspondence theory of truth. It may take one of two forms. The more general one questions whether "truth" has any meaning apart from verification and whether "correspondence" is a sufficiently definite characterization of it. The more special form questions whether any concrete methods of verification can be justified if one accepts a correspondence theory of truth. The next two chapters will be devoted to a more explicit statement of these dreaded skepticisms and an attempt to escape from them.

6

A Correspondence Theory of Truth

THE INTENTIONALISM we have been considering seems to lead, quite inescapably, to a correspondence theory of truth and even, in the case of perceptions, into a copy view: veridical perceptions somehow contain, as asserted of their objects, a selection of the very properties exemplified by those objects, and this constitutes their truth. We shall see presently that to describe this view as a "correspondence theory" is in some ways quite misleading and classifies it with positions strikingly dissimilar to it. However, if we were to put it along with coherence theories or with positions which reduce truth to verification, it would find itself in company even more foreign.

Now, if truth were some process of verification of that which is said to be true, or some coherence of it and certain other things (presumably things likewise said to be true), then we could have hopes of determining empirically, in some cases and to some degree, whether any specific thing claimed to be true is true. Not so, it would seem, if truth is correspondence. How can we ever tell whether any given perception is a copy of its object in the properties it selectively asserts—for the object remains ever outside it and any other perceptions we may experience?

This challenge will have to be met directly and in its own terms. First, however, let us note the strength of our position as against its competitors. The correspondence theory of truth in some broad way obviously accords with our everyday modes of thinking and speaking, whereas neither of its chief rivals does. When I say that it is true that my office clock is black, I mean that my office clock is black, that the statement, "My office clock is black," affirms something that actually is the case, that it agrees with the facts. I certainly do not mean that someone has verified it, will verify it, or is verifying it, or even that it could be verified if someone wished to take the trouble. Even more clearly I am not saying either that this judgment coheres with other judgments or that the fact it asserts fits into some harmonious pattern of facts which together compose a concordant universe.

The coherence theory is perhaps more easily disposed of, so let us turn first and very briefly to it. It is highly ambiguous, which may be one of its attractions. If we ask its advocates what it is the coherence of which constitutes truth, they sometimes talk as though it is statements asserting facts and at other times, the facts themselves. Now the latter interpretation openly violates common sense. It just may be, all appearances to the contrary notwithstanding, that the world is a perfect masterpiece, without an off-pitch fiddle, but no man in his right mind (that is, when not under the influence of some romantic metaphysics) claims that this is necessarily so by the very definition of "truth." When I swear in court relative to a claim made by the plaintiff that "She slapped his face" is a true statement, I am not swearing that the universe is one vast harmony in which just this element of human conflict makes its fitting contribution; rather, I am simply corroborating what the plaintiff asserted.

When the coherence theory is so formulated as to make truth a matter of the agreement of beliefs or statements with one another, its incompatibility with common sense is not so manifest. Indeed, it is very difficult to distinguish from the pragmatic view, particularly when that view identifies truth not with an actual process of verification but with a pattern of verifiability. Such a view can hardly fail to be attractive to empiricists, especially to those who, like myself, treat perceptions as statements and thus, if one were to accept the coherence theory, as elements in the harmony that constitutes truth. Nevertheless, as many thinkers have pointed out, our common thought makes it possible, however improbable, that the broadest and most coherent pattern of beliefs may be false; such a possibility does not contradict what we mean by truth. Indeed, we have historical instances of this in Ptolemaic astronomy and the wave theory of light, and if it be replied that these coherences were later discarded in favor of wider ones, we seem to be involved, if we take truth to be a concord of affirmations, in the consequence that truth changes, that the same statement, without any modification of meaning, can go from falsity to truth or vice versa. And this, most manifestly, does not accord with common thought (particularly if we note that verb tense is as relative to the time of utterance of a sentence as demonstratives in it, such as "here" or "there," are to its place). If Ptolemy was wrong about planetary motions he was wrong at the time he wrote the Almagest, not merely after the publication of the work of Copernicus, *On the Revolutions of the Heavenly Spheres*; or, put more properly, his theory was false without any reference to time—that is, if we go by ordinary thinking.

And an even more unfortunate commitment, from the standpoint of common sense, seems forced upon anyone adhering to the identification of truth with a concord of beliefs. Coherence is a matter of degree; truth, in the everyday acceptance, is all or none. Either the plaintiff's wife slapped him or she did not; so his claim that she did is either true or false. We may on occasion say of a statement that it is half true, but when we do, we mean to sound enigmatic or (as sometimes happens) to accept one part of a compound sentence but to reject another.

These last two unhappy features characterize as well the more radical pragmatic view that truth is the very process of verification. There is more and less verification, so truth must be a matter of degree. Moreover, as a process, verification comes and goes in time. James is absolutely right; on this view truth is something man-made—it occurs, like a birth or explosion. "Have you verified your statement?" literally means for James, "Have you made your statement true?" He thinks of truth as an event that happens in the biography of a belief, but in everyday life we do not look for a statement's truth as something that befalls the statement. The statement asserts a fact, for example, that a particularly large sunspot has recently appeared. Now we may wish to verify this; if we do, we cause certain other events to occur, such as looking at solar photographs. But it is important to note that these are new events about which no assertion was made in the statement whose truth we are seeking to verify. If we ask about the truth of statements affirming the existence of these new events, we are not asking about the truth of the statement about the sunspots, and their verification is quite a different matter, involving observations of people's behavior. This simply cannot be made to agree with the theory that truth is the process of verification. For one must grant with common sense that "A particularly large sunspot has recently appeared," "It is true that a particularly large sunspot has recently appeared" and "This last sentence is itself true" are all verified in exactly the same way, and they all assert one and the same fact, not a series of facts created by us as we seek in each case to verify the preceding statement.

Moreover, in everyday speech when we say that we believe some proposition, we mean that we accept it as true. According to the view we are criticizing, it would follow that we could never say that we believe some statement but do not believe that it has been verified or even perhaps that it ever will be, unless we are willing to contradict ourselves. For example, it would be quite improper to say, "I believe that the shock of his heart attack was the cause of hers, but this is probably one of those things that can never be verified."

Once more, our everyday assumption is that truth is built, so to speak, on meaning. A sentence to be true must have meaning, and, further, it is what is meant, supposing it to be as the sentence asserts, that somehow confers truth upon the sentence asserting it. Now if the truth of the sentence is some process of verifying it, then it would seem impossible to have a true sentence which is not about anything future to its utterance. Common sense would not tolerate the loss, as meaningless, of all sentences in the past tense or the timeless present, such as "It rained yesterday" and "Two and two make four." George Herbert Mead, a particularly courageous and stubborn pragmatist, has stood by the pragmatist position and claimed that we never do assert anything about the past, that when we appear to do so we are really affirming something about the future, namely, about those processes which, in ordinary parlance, would verify our statements. But his example is not to be recommended to any who would remain within the bounds of good sense.

It might be argued that at least some of the difficulty in the pragmatic theory does not arise from identifying truth with verification in particular, but rather from the fact that "truth" is defined, and that any view save that which makes truth ultimate and indefinable gets into similar trouble, for one can always sensibly ask about any character used to define "true" whether, in a given case, it is *true* that that character is exemplified, and this would lead to a vicious regress.   This, of course, applies if we define "truth" in terms of correspondence, as Frege, whom I am here following, has specifically pointed out.   Just as we can sensibly ask whether it is true that a certain sentence is verified and this does not amount to asking whether it is true that that sentence is true, so, it can be argued, we can as sensibly ask whether it is true that the sentence corresponds with the facts and this similarly does not amount to asking whether it is true that that sentence is true.

Personally, I am not convinced that there is a good parallel here, but in a certain sense Frege is correct, and by pointing out this sense we can find wherein the correspondence view has an advantage over the pragmatic and over every theory confusing truth with verification, and, moreover, we can gain an added insight into the correspondence theory itself.

To begin with, it is highly misleading to speak of truth as correspondence, for correspondence holds between classes whereas truth, if a relation at all, does not.   Russell has pointed out the necessity of a relation which will generate correspondence, say of the one-to-one type, a case in point being the-spouse-of in a monogamous society.   The generating relation holds between individuals, for example between Everett and Charlotte Hall, whereas the correspondence obtains between classes, say husbands and wives. The class of husbands is not, of course, the husband of the class of wives, nor is Everett in one-to-one correspondence with Charlotte.

Applying this to truth we see at once that it is not to be treated as a correspondence, say between true descriptive sentences and the facts they describe, for a class of sentences is not true, only individual ones are. If we use this terminology we must say that truth is a relation which generates correspondence; it is like husband-of, not the one-to-one correspondence of hubsands-wives. We may, and indeed I urge that we do, speak of the "truth-correspondence" relation (or better, the "truth-fact correspondence"), but in doing so we would be referring not to truth but to a relation it generates.

Nor are we to say, as some have interpreted the logical atomists to claim, that truth is a correspondence of the parts of a sentence to the parts of a fact. This view would require that the parts of a properly formulated sentence name constituents in the fact it asserts, and that its unity of names corresponds with the unity of what is named in the fact. This must be rejected if we follow the commonsensical grammar of "true." For a sentence to be true (or false) it must claim something (for example, that my desk-drawer sticks), and this is not reducible to a class of names, however correlated with a class of named entities, nor should it be confused with another claim, the claim that this set of names is so correlated. Nor will it do to use a correlation of names in the sentence with named constituents in the fact to set up a correlation between (true) sentences and facts, such that sentence and fact are paired by the circumstance of the one being composed of names which name the constituents of the other. For this again drops out the element of claim, of assertion, which is vital to the idea of truth in its commonsensical occurrence. Moreover, the correlation on this account would only obtain between sentences in an ideal language and the relevant facts, whereas a commonsensical approach demands the admission that many everyday statements (such as the example I just gave, that my desk-drawer sticks) are true as they stand.

Seeing this clearly, we are relieved of any feeling of compulsion to find some other relation, such as copying or picturing, to generate truth-correspondence; it is truth itself which does this.   Just as the correspondence between the classes, husbands and wives, is adequately set up by the relation husband-of (and its converse) holding between individuals, so that between true descriptions and facts described above is satisfactorily taken care of by truth itself.   Moreover, it would clearly be putting matters tail-end first to say that we should define "husband" in terms of the correspondence between the classes, husbands and wives, for the latter relation is, as Russell put it, generated by the former.   Similarly, it would be topsy-turvy to demand that we define truth by reference to the correspondence between true sentences and the facts they assert.   Very well, then, we must be careful to say not that truth is correspondence but that it generates a correspondence.

Understanding this, we are freed from the temptation to define "truth" by some arbitrary listing of true sentences or pairing of them with facts.   This consequence agrees with what many writers, sensitive to ordinary ways of thinking, have pointed out.   However, they have usually based their contention on the need of keeping "true" an open term, applicable to new sentences not at a given time formulated by anyone and so, a fortiori, not listed in any definition constructed at that time.   They have perfectly good grounds here for rejecting any such definition, but they are superficial; the fundamental difficulty lies deeper.   Suppose someone tried to define "husband" by enumerating all husbands or by pairing husbands and wives.   We could rightly object that this would not permit any new husbands to appear on the scene and therefore would clash with the openness of the term.   But we could invent a device that would keep our definition open: we could have the definition inscribed in a loose-leaf notebook in a public place and each new husband (and wife) could be required to place their names in this ever-expanding definition. Even in these circumstances it would run counter to common usage to say that this notebook would contain an acceptable definition of "husband" (or "spouse"), for the proffered definition would be in terms of a correlation of classes, not of the relation generating it. And something exactly similar can be said of any attempt to define "truth" in a like manner.

Perhaps a myth will help me make my point. There are innumerable worlds, not replicas of one another as some of the Greeks thought, but each different in kind. So for each possible, that is, self-consistent, world-hypothesis of every speculative metaphysician, no matter how bizarre, there is an actual world answering to it. Now, one of these worlds is so constructed that, whenever anyone in our world formulates in any fashion a true sentence, sounds, which would be taken for that sentence were anyone to hear them, blare forth from loudspeakers, and pictures, visual, auditory, olfactory or in any appropriate sensemode and appropriately formed structurally, are flashed on twenty-dimensional screens which, if anyone were to perceive them, could, granting sufficient intelligence on the part of the percipient, be apprehended as unique portrayals of just the facts asserted in the sentences previously mentioned. Strangely there are no people nor indeed any living organisms in this world, evolution, perhaps, having proceeded farther than on our planet. So, of course, there are no languages nor any language-users. Since I have allowed myself great latitude in composing my myth, I can perhaps avoid certain confusions by denying that there is any causal relation between events in our world and those just briefly described. The interesting phenomena mentioned can be ascribed to a "preestablished harmony" or perhaps better yet, not explained at all. Now, utilizing this cosmos some mathematical philosopher could work out a correlation between true assertions in our world and the facts they affirm by means of the sounds and pictures I have ascribed to that other world. This correlation would pair exactly the same statements and facts as our truth-correspondence does, and it would be an open correlation. Nevertheless it would not be truth nor would truth have been involved in its generation.

But if the same entities are correlated in the same way, do we not have the same correspondence-relation between the classes involved; for example, in our myth would we not have a genuine truth-correspondence between statements and facts although truth itself were by-passed in the generation of it? Perhaps this is a terminological issue, but I think I would like to answer in the negative. The consequence of course is that we must refuse not only to allow that a correspondence between sentences and facts can define truth but likewise to permit it to serve as a reliable mark or test of truth. Let me explain.

We may think of a correspondence between classes (say a one-to-one correlation) in a more or less abstract way, or, to use W. E. Johnson's terminology, as a determinable, or, again, as some determinate falling under it. Imagine a Japanese family ready to eat their evening meal. Each member, we will suppose, has his own personal chopsticks appropriately placed before him. We can, in these circumstances, correlate individuals and chopsticks by means of either of two relations, ownership or setting. Do these not generate the same correlation? They do if we are thinking of correlation as a determinable; they do not if we have in mind determinate forms. In one sense, then, the ownership-correspondence is the same as the location-correspondence between persons and chopsticks; in another, it is not. Suppose the family has a new maid and she is unacquainted with the ownership relation; then to speak of the correlation set up by the locations as an ownership-correspondence would be misleading: the same people would be correlated with the same chopsticks but not as owners of them. Now let us return to our myth. The same sentences could be correlated with the same facts by our ingenious mathematician as by the truth-relation, but it would be misleading to call that correlation a truth-correspondence, for it is not as true of their correlated facts that the sentences are in correspondence with the facts, but as occurrences having the peculiar properties described in our fable and thus appropriately paired by our mathematician.

But now even though truth and even perhaps the truth-variety of correspondence it generates be unique and thus in a sense indefinable, may they not be characterized and even characterized so as to mark them off from other unique forms of correspondence? To some extent I think this is possible and I shall try very briefly and with misgivings to do it.

The determinate correspondence which truth generates is peculiar in that one of its sets of terms (Russell would call it the "domain"—I refer to the entities said to be true) is not a collection of existents as such, but of intentions. At the level of perception, it is composed not of the perceptions as events and as characterized by their own properties (the time of their occurrence, their place in someone's personal biography and so on) but of them as assertions containing properties as experienced (the properties they ascribe to their objects).

A second peculiarity is that the other set of terms between which truth-correspondence holds (Russell would call it the "converse-domain"—I refer to the facts asserted by true propositions) contains items which do not exist. The admission of negative facts, of non-exemplification of certain properties by particular individuals, may appear strange but I do not see how to avoid it if one accepts the truth of any negative judgments. These peculiarities show that the correlation which truth sets up is not properly conceived as a correlation between things that exist or things *as* existent. This does not, however, prohibit our thinking of it as a correspondence.

Now it might be objected that truth should not be treated as a relation of any kind, for we do not in everyday speech formulate it relationally. We say that Charlotte Hall is the wife of Everett Hall or that 4 is the square of 2, but we do not say that "The tablecloth is dirty" is true of the tablecloth's being dirty or if we do it sounds strange because so obviously redundant; when we use "true" at all it has the appearance of a quality-predicate rather than a relation. We do at least occasionally speak of a sentence as true (if, for example, we wish to corroborate a statement made by someone else), and when we do, "true" appears to characterize the sentence by itself, not to relate it to something else. Yet a moment's thought reveals that it is not a quality-word. If someone says that the tablecloth is dirty we may look at the tablecloth to see if it is, but if anyone asserts that the sentence, "The tablecloth is dirty," is true we do not turn to the sentence to observe whether it is true but rather to the dirty tablecloth. And in doing so we seem tacitly to admit that truth is a relation, for we look to the factual correlate to determine whether the sentence asserting it is true (I am here speaking loosely in everyday terms; I think I could put my point in intentional categories).

I admit that, if we bear these peculiarities in mind, it might be best not to speak of truth as a relation at all. Certainly it is strikingly dissimilar to the relation between a photograph and what it pictures, for each of these relata are existent entities. One might even be tempted to classify the view I am outlining, particularly at the perceptual level, as "monistic" rather than "dualistic," and this would in some degree be fitting. One could think of it in terms of E. B. Holt's searchlight analogy and speak of veridical perception as "selecting" certain features of physical things, remembering that light (unlike perception considered as intentional) is physical and has effects upon its objects. But this will not do, either. For we must remember that there are true negative sentences, at least in our conventional language, and there are their perceptual originals of the sort I have tried to portray in an earlier chapter. To carry Holt's metaphor through, therefore, would require a companion to his searchlight which we might call a "search-dark" which by the darkness it throws upon something correctly reveals features that are not there.

Trying to strike a balance, I am still inclined towards speaking of truth as "correspondence," particularly if it is constantly borne in mind that it is a very special sort of correspondence, of its own unique kind, and that truth is not strictly the correspondence itself but a relation which generates it. We do not, then, have a definition of truth but we do have a characterization of it. Are we any better off than people who hold other theories, specifically those who would identify truth with verification? I think we are, and precisely in a way which Frege's objection now helps point up. If it is asked of us whether, in a case of admittedly veridical perceptions, it is true that the perceptions correspond with the facts (in just the determinate form of correspondence required), we can see that the question is redundant, like asking whether it is true that it is true, in a way in which it is not redundant to ask whether an admittedly true belief is verified (or is being verified or even merely can be verified).

7

A Coherence Theory of Verification

OUR PROBLEM is this: if truth be a relation generating a correspondence between our factual assertions and the facts they assert, how can we ever tell when a sentence possesses it? We earlier set aside the more general forms of this problem, but we must now deal with it concretely. What kind or kinds of verification can the individual sentences forming the basis of our knowledge of fact have if their truth consists in a relation they bear to objects which they intend but do not literally contain?

Here we may borrow from a competitor. Although coherence will not do as a definition of truth, it does serve as a suggestion concerning methods of verification. But this use of it brings immediately to mind certain objections we had against it as a theory of truth.

One of these was that the most coherent and comprehensive set of factual statements might be false. Now this possibility I propose we accept as a risk we constantly take in trying to know about our world. It should be noted that this introduces no contradiction here as it did when coherence functioned as a definition of truth, although it does prohibit any final claim of certainty for any knowledge of fact.

But now we must face a form of this objection which does quite definitely have a bearing on our use of coherence. Let us put it as Russell has: if individual sentences have no probability, coherent sets of them will not yield any; thus we cannot verify to any degree the truth of any given statement by appeal to its coherence with other statements if these others themselves gain all their verification in a like manner. I quite agree with Russell. Metaphors about sticks that support one another by leaning against one another in a circle will not suffice. We must break the circle somewhere and I suggest that we do it everywhere.

I mean by this that we take individual sentences forming the basis of our factual knowledge as each having its own inherent probability. To what sentences do I allude? I refer to all actual perceptions. Each of these by the fact of its occurrence is to be considered as worthy in some degree of acceptance as true. For reasons to which allusion has already been made, we can extend this basis, with proper caution, to conventional proxies not as statements in their own right but as translations of, and thus substitutes for, their perceptual originals. The degree of this probability cannot properly be formulated in quantitative terms; obviously neither a frequency ratio resting on empirical counting nor an a priori calculation presupposing equal probabilities can be applied here. The best we can do, perhaps, is to say that every actual perception has some inherent probability lying somewhere between nullity and certainty.

What are my grounds for this assignment of inherent probability to all actual perceptions? Certainly not that they may be presumed due to the stimulation of sense organs. Such a procedure would constitute a far more vicious circle than the one composed of sticks which I mentioned a short while ago, since it would be hidden. What evidence have we that there are sense organs and that they are on various occasions stimulated? Only that offered by our perceptions.

To be honest, I must admit that we have no further grounds within our system for assigning this inherent probability to perceptions. It does not follow from anything else already given or more basic than it. As far as knowledge of fact is concerned, inherent probability is an essential part of the basis and constitutes ground for further assertions, in the form of generalized statements, built upon it.

This does not mean that it is simply an item of faith or arbitrary decision. It is, as I see it, integral to our whole intentional approach and shares with that approach whatever plausibility the latter may have. And we can claim a rather large plausibility for empirical intentionalism, namely, a greater agreement with actual thought and practice in everyday and scientific pursuits than that displayed by any rival epistemology. I have elsewhere tried to distinguish between what serves as basic *within* a philosophical system and what functions as a basis *of* the system. The basis of the system developed in this book is to be found in the categories of everyday speech and thought, and the forms of our ordinary experience as molded by them. On this basis we must take the claims of our perceptions seriously. When I have the perceptual experience of a yellow pencil on the table before me I am to assume that there probably is a yellow pencil on the table before me.

Perhaps an analogy will help. In the American legal system, following the English in principle, there are various rules of evidence of a man's guilt. If someone is on trial for having committed a crime, his lawyers will attempt to confute the evidence which the state brings against him or to have it disallowed by the court. But suppose a curious spectator from the continent should ask, "I notice that there is evidence against him and attempts to meet it, but where is the evidence in favor of him? Everyone seems to suppose him innocent, since he has not pleaded guilty, until proved otherwise." The appropriate answer would be, "Exactly. This is basic in our whole system, that a man is assumed to be innocent until proved to be guilty." So in our empirical intentionalism a perception is to be assumed reliable until shown to be otherwise.

Now, what sort of evidence can be brought to bear against the assertion constituting any given perception? Clearly only that presented by other, conflicting perceptions or generalizations based upon them. And we are justified in pronouncing a perception to be (most probably) incorrect in some respect only if some other perception, conflicting with it in this respect, is more coherent with the whole body of relevant perceptions.

This brings us back to another objection we had to coherence as a theory of truth. It was that "coherence" is a vague term. We pointed out an ambiguity in its use about what is to cohere. This we can now eliminate by specifying that it is perceptions of the same object that are to cohere. But now another ambiguity must be faced which we did not mention before. What is it to cohere? Something more than logical consistency is required. Indeed, for a purist perceptions cannot be inconsistent since, strictly speaking, they contain no negatives. But even on our less rigorous treatment, formal consistency of a set of perceptions is not sufficient to give appreciable additional probability to that inherent in each of them. On the other hand, we want no nebulous commitment, however high-minded, to a heavenly harmony or for that matter to any prior predication concerning the universe: the world is, by and large, as we perceive it, with all its blemishes and discord. We seek no coherence of fact but of statements of fact. What is this to be and where can we find it?

Let us turn to the latter half of our question first. We shall find what we want in the actual practices of everyday

life and of scientific habit. Although we do, in these capacities, accept individual perceptions very largely at face
value, some are discounted or even rejected as counterfeit,
while others are eagerly sought, precisely on the basis of
the better or worse coherences which they present. And I
use the plural advisedly. Coherence is no one simple thing
here but a plurality of patterns. I cannot hope to investigate or even to mention all of them. I shall take a few as
typical and important, emphasizing that I am, essentially,
just articulating our ordinary, uncriticized practices.   I
shall then indicate how they fit the empirical intentionalism
to which we are committed. The alert observer will note
that, following common sense, generalizations are tacitly
introduced here at the very basis of our knowledge of fact.
I postpone for later consideration the problem which this
involves.

Let us start with any particular perception. Its inherent
probability may be increased, decreased or left unmodified
as we relate it to other perceptions. Consider the last
possibility. Other perceptions leave the inherent probability of a given one unchanged if they are irrelevant to it,
and they are irrelevant if they do not have any objects the
same as its own. Two perceptions have a common object
when they describe the same particular in some one respect.
In thinking about the empirical negative we have already
found grounds for suspecting that any attempt to define or
even to specify unequivocally what is meant by the phrase,
"in some one respect," would lead to difficulties if it did not
end in complete failure. I can do very little more with it
here.

The phrase obviously concerns predications and almost
as clearly it is a way of classifying them. Going beyond
this is difficult but necessary. Perhaps we could say that
predications are in the same respect if either they are the

same or, if different, might, at least in some instances, be naturally considered to be rivals, to be incompatible if made of the same particular. Thus to predicate yellow and red of my pencil is to predicate of it in some one respect but to predicate yellow and hard is not. Here we are in trouble, both about where to draw the line and about how to clarify the expression, "might be naturally considered," when we say that two different predications are in the same respect if they might be naturally considered to be incompatible if made of the same individual. Although I may be thought a coward, I shall, confronted with these difficulties, simply refer back to my earlier remarks about the empirical negative as giving sufficient clues about how we should deal with them.

But now we must face a further problem and one from which we cannot flee even for the moment. To state it requires that we make another distinction, one which we shall find useful and indeed vital later, as well as now. Two perceptions unquestionably have no bearing upon one another's inherent probability if they have no object whatever in common. If I am observing a spider crawling along its web towards a fly and you are listening with closed eyes to a Beethoven quartet, our perceptions are mutually irrelevant. But suppose you and I both perceive my yellow pencil, but I, grasping it, feel it to be cool whereas your perception contains no thermal predication of it. Our perceptions then have an object in common, the pencil as yellow, and in this respect yours is corroborative of mine, but in respect to coolness, yours is irrelevant to mine and thus does not affect its inherent probability.

This leads me to advise that we never speak of the probability of a perception as a whole (or in any case only rarely, as when we reject an experience as a dream or as completely hallucinatory) but always only in some respect.

Looking ahead, let me say that our coherence patterns will sometimes allow us to say that a perception may have high probability in some respects and low in others.

And now we must make another distinction, but in this case a very commonplace one. Suppose instead of my pencil we both observe my blotter, I seeing it as white with black printing on it, you, as blue with some darker blue stains. Instead of being in conflict, these perceptions might be irrelevant to one another in respect to color if I am looking at one side (the printed) and you are seeing the other (the absorbent). Our perceptions in this instance do not predicate differing colors of the same particular, for different parts of the same particular are different particulars.

In passing, we should note that the perceptions just mentioned might reinforce one another as regards the shape, size and location of the blotter, for these are whole-properties.

It is evident that the question whether two perceptions are relevant in some specified respect is not always easily answered; indeed, we can never be certain that a pair of perceptions do predicate even of the same particular. The subjects of predication never bodily enter our perceptions— the grasshopper never hops into our experience of it. We identify the individuals we perceive by groups or patterns of predications to be found in our perceptions. Whenever there are conflicts in these it is always possible that the perceptions involved are of different things. I think we do assume in everyday life the identity of indiscernibles in the sense that no two individuals have all the same properties (including their spatial and temporal relations); in any case we operate roughly on the principle that the likelihood that two perceptions are of the same thing increases as the number of properties they assert in common increases, al-

though the presence of rare properties or patterns of properties may complicate this relation (consider, for example,
how we determine whether we are looking at the same man
in a crowd: "The man I'm observing is near the middle,"
"Yes," "Is bald," "Yes," "Wears a blue suit," "Yes," "With
a red tie," "Yes" "And there, he is lighting a cigarette,"
"Yes, yes—the very one I'm watching").

As just mentioned, two perceptions which at first appear
relevant may turn out not to be so, if, for example, we can
take them as being about different particular things. Contrariwise, a pair that might seem, at least on our analysis up
to this point, to be irrelevant may be relevant. Here I have
in mind that our actual everyday practice, which may not
stand up against the most rigorous scientific standards of
observation, nevertheless is "good enough" for many purposes. Suppose I literally experience my pencil to be
smooth—I am holding it as I write. I report this to you
and you say, "Why yes, I can see that it is smooth." How
can you say this? You see it is yellow but can you see
that it is smooth? So challenged you answer, "I don't exactly see its smoothness, but it is enameled and shiny; I see
reflections on it I wouldn't if it were rough." Pushing this
a little further, I think we can say that you have tacitly
generalized, you have allowed habit, as built up by your
previous perceptual experience, to come in without the
presence of conventional symbols. Whenever, in seeing
something highly reflective, you have also touched it, you
have felt it to be smooth. So this pattern of highlights,
without the intervention of conventional words, has come
to carry with it the predication of smoothness. Whether
or not we admit this sort of thing in the region we call
"pure perceptions" is perhaps not too important—it frequently occurs and certainly for ordinary purposes has a
bearing on the inherent probability of individual percep-

tions when these are brought into reaction with one another. A few other examples are our "seeing" the sweating glass of beer to be cool and the steaming tea to be hot, or our "hearing" the screeching bicycle to be approaching and the clanging bell to be struck by its clapper.

These cases of "vicarious" predication, as I shall call them, differ from conventional ones to be found in proxies because they introduce no new objects for perception whose purpose is to carry the predication.   The presence of a property or a pattern of properties asserted in its own right of the thing perceived is made, through habit, to carry the predication of some other property not, as I shall say, "personally present" in the perception.   The highlights are literally seen on the pencil although they also, through habit, function to assert the smoothness; and so for the steam in relation to the warmth of the tea.

I think in general I am being true to scientific procedure and certainly to everyday practice if I say that perceptions that predicate vicariously of the same individual in some one respect as does a given perception are relevant to the inherent probability of the latter, but less so, that is, modify its inherent probability less than do other perceptions that predicate personally of that same individual in the respect concerned.   Take a single example: I grasp the beer-glass without looking at it and feel it to be warm.   You "see" it, by its sweating, to be cool.   A friend, to settle our differences, touches it and he finds it cool.   I would find his disagreement with my experience more telling than yours (I am considering them separately; their corroboration of course adds weight to each).

We are not quite done with complications even yet. Your perception and his come to me as proxies, mine appears in its own right.   In general, as we have seen, proxies introduce sources of error not to be found in perceptions themselves. In the case just given, I might look at the glass myself and feel it with my other hand. By and large, proxies for perceptions have less bearing on the probability of a perception than do other relevant perceptions.

Let us turn to perceptions themselves and what they "personally" predicate. For any given respect in which it describes its object, every perception has an inherent probability of being correct. Other perceptions ostensibly of the same object may add to or detract from that probability. Let us start with the former.

Suppose I am anxiously watching at dusk for the sail of Boysterous, returning from a cruise with Richard and his friend, Bruce. "There she is!" I exclaim, putting into words my perceptual experience. "That's our boat, all right," my wife agrees. "You are correct," adds Bruce's father, giving further confirmation. This pattern of coherence I shall call "quantitative corroboration" and of it state as follows: roughly, the larger the number of perceptions of some particular thing or event agreeing with a given one in a certain respect, that is, predicating of it the same property or constellation of properties, the higher the probability of that one, the rate of increase in probability going down as the number of corroborating perceptions goes up.

Let us change the circumstances in our example a little. My wife, instead of being on the dock with me, is watching from the cottage some distance away, and Bruce's father is on the tower on Eagle Bluff. Both have agreed to wave white cloths when they see Boysterous. Just about the time I discern the ship's characteristic sail-outline they wave their cloths. In this case I would feel that their corroborative experience gave greater confirmation than under the first arrangement, justifying my feeling by the consideration that, if I had misperceived, my companions would be more likely to fall into the same error to the extent that they were observing under the same conditions as I. This is supported by the common assumption that just looking again is not as good as looking from a different angle or under other circumstances. We must be cautious here (as with all our statements of coherence, since often different patterns conflict); a set of perceptions under similar "ideal conditions" might yield larger confirmation than another of the same number under more various circumstances. Moreover, as we vary the circumstances we make it more difficult to determine whether we are perceiving the same individual. We must keep in mind that neither what we observe nor the conditions under which we observe enter our perceptions physically; they are there only as perceived. Ideally they constitute different objects so that as we change the one (the conditions) we may preserve the other (what is under observation). But ordinarily this is not possible. In the example last given, Bruce's father would see the sails as having a somewhat different contour from their appearance to me.

With these and indeed other qualifications in mind, I formulate the coherence-pattern we are now considering, which I call "corroboration by supplemental difference," as follows: on the average and up to the point at which an identification of the object is in jeopardy, agreeing perceptions of something in some respect yield greater confirmation to the extent that they occur in a context of differing predications of other things, or of the same thing in other respects. Bruce's father sees Boysterous' sails against the background of Horseshoe Island; I, against the gap between the island and Shanty Point. To him, by this contrast, they seem almost white; to me, looking toward the western sky, they are almost black. These very differences, providing we can identify the characteristic cut of the boat's sails, add

greater corroboration than if our perceptions were essentially just replicas of one another.

I want now to shift for a moment to perceptions that
disagree in order to bring out a pattern of coherence which
can equally be used, as of course all these patterns can, to
show either an increase or a decrease in probability when
we relate a single perception to others. Whenever we have
two perceptions which disagree, predicating incompatible
properties of the same thing, each lowers the inherent probability of the other in the respect in which there is disagreement; they need not do so equally, however. In this comparison one may remain more probable than the other providing it is more discriminative in the respect involved.
Suppose I look at Mount Hiei first at a distance, when she
appears a rather uniform bluish-gray through the haze, and
then from her foot, when her autumnal colors are immense-
ly variegated. I would quite naturally in ordinary life assume that the closer view was more reliable concerning her
colors than the more distant. As regards her shape, however, I would presume that the view from Kyoto was better
than that from the cablecar as I start the ascent. In the
former case the principle of "maximum discrimination"
seems obviously at work; in the latter, it might be questioned. I think that as regards shape we do have another
principle operating as well, the one I called "quantitative
corroboration," for I would no doubt be unconsciously
bringing to bear the knowledge that there is much more
agreement on the mountain's over-all shape on the part of
those seeing her from a distance than of those on her sides.
Still, I think the principle of discrimination also contributes
positively in this case.

Consider what we mean by this principle. If one perception is to be more discriminative in some respect than
another, it must predicate more properties of a given kind—

and thus possibly incompatible ones—of the same particular thing. This it can only do by discriminating more parts; otherwise conflicting properties would be ascribed by the perception to some one thing. A greater discrimination of parts allows not merely a larger number of predications in a given respect but a greater degree of distinction between part-properties, whole-properties and unbroken properties. This should be clear enough when applied to the colors of Mount Hiei. The closer view differentiates more part-properties (the reds of the maples, greens of the conifers, browns of rocks and clumps of straw) as contrasted with the unbroken property (a bluish-gray) of the distant prospect. But what about shape? Any observation obtained going up the mountain discloses as many shapes of her parts, perhaps more, than a view from the city, but the shape of the whole and indeed the shapes of many of the larger parts are omitted, and shape is a whole-property in a way in which color is not.

If I had not wanted to contrast the results of applying our principle of maximum discrimination to predications in different respects I could have used the following pair: the perception of Mount Hiei from the same location but once on a clear day and once during a rainstorm. We would probably admit better discrimination both of color and shape in the first than in the second of these.

Now, if we allow generalization to come in, we are in a fair way to understand many of our ordinary and scientific preferences for some perceptions as against other, disagreeing ones. We almost always assume that those perceptions which occur under conditions generally resulting in greater discrimination in a given respect are more reliable than their competitors. So for the determination of colors we choose white light; for reading ordinary print, a distance of perhaps half a meter, but for a large sign, several meters;

for discerning intra-cellular structure, a microscope but for the conformation of our hand, the naked eye. Take the well-worn instance of the coin, or rather of the shape of its face. Philosophers of all persuasions have generally been honest about this. In daily commerce with it we believe the coin to be round, not elongated. The reason seems clear; although we seldom see it round, when we do, our perception is under ideal conditions for discriminating shape, namely, our line of vision is at right angles to the shape in question. As we move away from this and towards a line of regard in the same plane as the coin's surface, our discrimination is lessened until the surface completely disappears.

And under these generalizations about better conditions for perceptual discrimination should be placed those about individual observers. For colors, we put aside the observations of the color-blind; for shape, those who suffer from astigmatism; for musical intonation, people who are tone-deaf. And training, too, comes in. In fine scientific work, one must know what to look for, but even in non-scientific pursuits, acquaintance with and interest in discrimination of perceivable qualities or relations improves capacities. A painter's color observations are more reliable than a non-painter's. Charlotte Hunt, research specialist for General Foods Corporation, has compiled a list of terms used by professional coffee tasters. It contains words for twenty-eight discriminable coffee flavors. Why are these men paid for their services? Obviously because, concerning tastes, there often is dispute, and theirs are deemed more reliable than the general run (in respect, of course, to coffee flavors).

The word "reliable" in this context is not free from ambiguity. It may mean, "is likely to fit patterns of regularity in the occurrence of other perceptions," whereas I have been using it in the sense, "is probably correct in predication of properties." Not that these meanings are wholly unrelated. Common sense and science both operate on the assumption that nature is, by and large, uniform. If we, as philosophers, accept this procedural commitment as something not merely justified by our perceptual experience but also in its turn contributive to the determination of the relative probabilities of various conflicting perceptions, as I think we should, then we have another coherence pattern of confirmation. If in applying it we look simply to the future, we might designate it, "the principle of predictive power," but if, as we ought to do, we think of it more widely, "the postulate of regularity" would perhaps be a better name for it. In the case of two disagreeing observations it has us assign the greater probability to the one which fits more regularities in other observed events.

This usually agrees with our other criteria. For example, the greater discriminative capacity of the professional coffee taster agrees with his more frequent success in spotting where the coffee was grown than that of an amateur in this area. Indeed, this agreement is so striking that it may add plausibility to a phenomenalistic transformation of our whole account of perceptual corroboration. I can conceive a phenomenalist's acceptance of our coherence patterns, but not as tests of the probable correctness of perceptions, since he rejects our intentionalism. Rather, they are to be used as aids, found generally trustworthy, in predicting future experience or more generally in putting experience into regular sequences. He would point out that if one perception is similar to a greater number of others in some respect, particularly if in other respects it differs more or if it is more discriminative than another which in ordinary life is treated as conflicting with it, we are then justified by past experience in considering it a more reliable basis for predicting future experience.

The issue here runs deeper than this matter of modes of confirmation of individual perceptions; it involves a comparison of phenomenalism and intentionalism as total systems. Nevertheless, there are considerations that have bearing on the larger subject. The phenomenalist would need to make the other criteria subsidiary to that of regularity, and thus always to yield to it when in conflict with it. This does not, I believe, accord with our actual thought and practice.

The famous Michelson-Morley experiment tremendously increased the observers' powers of discriminating different velocities (of light in and across the direction of the earth's motion). Its results did not agree with the laws of motion. Einstein, as a good scientist, accepted these results in preference to those obtained under conditions not allowing equally fine discrimination. It might be retorted that Einstein immediately began searching for other uniformities and eventually succeeded in finding one (to replace the parallelogram law for compound motions). True, but he undertook the search; he assumed that the greater discrimination provided by the conditions set up by Michelson and Morley gave more reliable results concerning actual velocities. Science, I conceive, stands ever ready, although perhaps always reluctant, to throw out laws that conflict with suitably established probabilities using the other criteria I have mentioned (quantitative corroboration, corroboration by supplemental difference and, above all, maximum discrimination). Not that it never chooses the postulate of uniformity when that principle conflicts with others, but it does not choose it consistently, as though the others were wholly subsidiary to it, mere cues of it or substitutes for it. It operates, that is, as though the final consideration were not the laws one can formulate but the actual properties and relations of events.

And in this it agrees with common sense. To speak for the latter, let me add to a myth I presented in an earlier chapter. One of the many worlds that exist is exactly like ours save for one fact—all of its observers are totally color-blind. To compensate for this, they have developed a mechanism containing a sort of photoelectric cell much like our exposure meter for photography which allows them to read off on a black and white scale the color of whatever they look at. This device gives them as great a power of prediction, of finding color-uniformities, as we of normal eyesight possess. Is it commonsensical to say that their black and white perceptions give them as good a picture of the way things are as do our black and white and variously colored? I think not.

The list of coherence-patterns just presented is not meant to be exhaustive. It is, I think, representative and contains some of the most important ones, but its purpose is illustrative, namely, to show how a correspondence theory of truth, as involved in empirical intentionalism, might be united with a coherence theory of verification based upon actual practices in science and daily life.

A question arises concerning conflicts between coherence-patterns, for although these patterns frequently agree with one another when concretely applied, they sometimes lead in opposite directions, as when the larger number of corroborating observations favors one perception but the greater discriminative capacity of the observer, another. Do we have any ranking of the relative authority of our principles of perceptual corroboration? My answer, again relying on actual practice, is "No, not in general. Different kinds of cases are handled differently, according to the circumstances." This may seem unsatisfactory since it appears to make a vast amount of factual "knowledge" depend upon arbitrary decision which can vary from person to person. To some extent this is true and is the price we must pay for taking common sense rather than our instinct for logical neatness as our guide. But decisions in this matter are not completely ad hoc. For one thing, no one of the verificational principles is allowed to assume absolute authority, so that irrespective of the strength of the evidence on other principles and the weakness of its own, the decision can (reasonably) favor it when in conflict with the others. For example, there is a place where greater discrimination must yield to a larger number of corroborating observations when these principles give opposite results, although there is no standard rule about its location. Also, we commonly defer to people of judgment and experience in the area involved—their decisions are accepted in preference to the novice's even though they are a matter of art and not of formula. But most important, we must bear in mind that the decisions of which we now speak are about relative probabilities, not "knowledge" in some absolute sense logically implying the truth of that which is properly said to be known.

In passing, let me call attention to the fact that, although the word "knowledge" occurs in the general title of this volume, I have nowhere in it undertaken a review of the various uses to which the English verb, "know," and its derivatives are put. This would be an interesting empirical investigation, but one for the professional linguist, not the philosopher. It follows, of course, that I have not engaged in the more theoretical inquiry, which must be based on the results of the investigation mentioned, whether there is any common factor in these uses. Up to this point I have taken "knowledge of fact" in one of its common meanings and tried to explore, not the expression and its use, but what it is commonly taken to designate, particularly at its basic and irreducible minimum, and I have subjected it to analysis and criticism. I project the same for "knowledge of value." If anyone objects to my title, I offer him, without recommendation, the substitute, "The Epistemological Bases of Probabilities Concerning Fact and Value."

One important office of decision is in determining the role to be allowed well-established laws when these are in conflict with probabilities assigned on other criteria. This is directly involved in the use of the postulate of regularity, but it is present in the application of other coherence-patterns as well, as I pointed out specifically in the case of generalizations about the best conditions for maximizing discrimination. I have nothing to add about decision here, but I would like to insert a word about the fact that decision in favor of well-founded laws is sometimes allowed, for this introduces generalizations into the very bedrock of empirical knowledge, thereby destroying, it would seem, the firmness of the whole structure. It will be noted, however, that this is no new crack suddenly appearing in the foundations of our system; it was involved as far back as our acceptance of proxies for perceptions, especially for negative ones. Although it should give us some concern, it does not show a fatal defect. First, individual perceptions themselves, in their purest form, do not possess certainty, so the introduction of regularity as a desideratum does not take it away. Second, the laws we are speaking of are not a priori; they have their evidence not in themselves but in perceptions upon which they are generalizations. Consequently, they are never beyond invalidation by further perceptions. Third, their role here is not the destruction of the inherent probability of any perception taken singly, but the adjustment of perceptual probabilities to one another. Fourth, we are only being honest to actual practice when we refuse to go back to a level of experience completely devoid of generalization.

Granting all this, however, we still must face the truth that in the introduction of regularity at the basis of factual knowledge we have an assumption which is irreducible to inherent probability of individual, ungeneralized perceptions. This assumption is that nature is more likely to be regular than not. Perhaps it will help us accept this principle at the lowest level to note that, if it is not granted here, it must be postulated higher up in order to justify the leap in all induction. I shall not add my voice to the dissension on this matter; I am happy to say that, having chosen categories of everyday thought as the extra-philosophical ground of our whole epistemological system, we are left no alternative to the acceptance of induction as a principle, though not to any particular generalization as a valid instance.

If this appeal to common sense is satisfactory for the postulate of regularity and our other coherence-patterns of perceptual corroboration so far as presupposing the lawfulness of events is concerned, will not something similar do for these patterns in their specific diversity of character? I think so. We need not be too disturbed by the skeptic's challenge, "If truth be a relation between experience and something extra-experiential, how can coherence-patterns of experience have any bearing, even that of mild probability, upon it?" for every philosophical system rests on categorial assumptions which for it are beyond question, and in the strife of such systems the only really firm neutral ground is that found in the categories of everyday thought. The epistemological position outlined in these chapters is commonsensical both in its intentionalism as regards meaning and truth and in its acceptance of coherence as regards verification. If it be objected that one could have an epistemology involving fewer categorial assumptions, I would be inclined to agree, but would ask, "On what grounds are we to prefer the simpler, in this sense, to the more complex?" The answer is not self-evident nor a priori. If it be asserted that common sense is involved in contradiction when it combines the categorial assumptions mentioned, I would reply with a flat denial: they may be independent but they do not conflict.

However, I should like to qualify this last admission. Although an intentionalist theory of meaning and truth and a coherence theory of verification are independent logically, neither strictly implying the other, they do have an appropriateness to one another which adds to the plausibility of their combination. Take the principle of quantitative corroboration. If we accept the intentionalistic account of experience outlined earlier, it is reasonable to suppose that there can be a multiplicity of perceptions of the same external object. If so, when in agreement, they can bear one another out. Consider corroboration by supplemental difference. If there is an external world about which our perceptual experience may be in error and if that experience itself occurs under conditions in that same external world, it is reasonable to suppose that a multiplicity of perceptions agreeing in some respect but differing in others enhance one another's probability more than an equal number that are more completely alike. Finally, think about maximum discrimination. If the predications made in perception are to the effect that the properties personally present in perception are exemplified more concretely, that is, along with a much larger number of properties, by the external thing, then it is reasonable to suppose that we have come closer to the full nature of that thing in any given respect as our perception is more discriminative in that respect.

We have completed our exploration of factual knowledge. In it we have left aside all problems of inductive generalization, confining our attention as far as possible to the basis of our knowledge of fact in individual perceptions. The reasons for this are that the author has nothing to contribute to the literature on the topic of inductive logic and that one's philosophical position is pretty much determined by the direction one takes at the primary level of perceptual experience.

This account must balance when taken by itself. But it surely is not in its disfavor if it lends support to a strikingly parallel account rendered of our knowledge of value. For a most impartial judgment, the two should be read together and in relation, not separately. Part II is thus not wholly irrelevant to the subject we have considered in Part I of this book.

Part II. Our Knowledge of Value

8

The Intentionalism of
Emotive Language

THINKING BACK over Part I, I realize that it contains
some things that may look strange to fellow philosophers in England and the United States. However, in the
main, I think the intentional empiricism there portrayed is
not altogether foreign to contemporary Anglo-American
philosophical circles. Phenomenalism and positivism are
rapidly losing strength in the face of a widespread recognition that everyday speech is "physicalistic" and that, presumably, everyday thought about the world is objective,
not subjective, is about external things and events, not
internal experiences or sense-data. But a similar remark
cannot be made about discussions of value, although ordinary language appears to be just as objective when the
subject is morals as when it is facts. The tendency among
our contemporary philosophers is to "interpret" common
speech-forms so that when one says, for example, that
racial discrimination is wrong, it turns out that one is asserting nothing whatever about racial discrimination or in
any case that one is not claiming that it is wrong.

I must qualify this characterization somewhat, for there
is a growing recognition that the positivistic scrapping of
all value-talk as "non-sense" cannot be harmonized with an
analysis that remains true to the spirit and meaning of
everyday speech. The most recent tendency is to try to

close the gap between a positivistic account and the obvious intent of ordinary value-language without taking the final step of admitting that often when we say that something is not as it ought to be we mean that it is not as it ought to be. This partial closure is accomplished by pointing out how various are the uses to which everyday speech is put and, in the sphere of moral talk, by stressing its utilization to influence people's behavior and to offer them guidance in coming to decisions.   So we have much discussion about what constitutes a "good reason" and even a good "moral" reason for doing or refraining from some action, without ever admitting that the goodness or rightness of the action forms the best and most obvious reason for doing it and the contrary characters for refraining from it.   The assumption still appears to be that somehow it is nonsense to assert any value.   Now this assumption simply does not square with common thought and speech.

Perhaps a bit of fiction will help me make my point.

Frank and George had just come from Sunday worship in a Protestant church in a small university town in southern United States.

"Wasn't Jones's sermon great?" asked Frank.

"I'll admit it was very moving, Frank."

"I know how deeply segregationist you are, George, but didn't our minister's plea to remember that all people are children of God and thus of one family change your attitude?"

"Yes it did, Frank.   I still think Negroes are inferior in native ability to whites, but Jones pointed out rightly that God loves those of lesser intelligence as much as those of greater, and that we, his children, should do the same."

"Well, that's a great admission coming from you, George.   By the way, do you know my friend Smith, the philosopher?"

"I'm glad to join you, if you don't mind," said Smith. "I couldn't help overhearing your conversation and as I'm interested in the logic of concepts in our practical discourse I'd like to try my analysis to see what you think of it."

"Go right ahead," George replied. "I must confess I'm a bit puzzled myself about how Jones in twenty minutes changed my attitude so profoundly."

"Well, what do you think of this? You are accustomed to having people condemn you, tell you that hate and prejudice are wrong and unchristian. This arouses an antagonistic attitude in you."

"You're absolutely right."

"But Jones started differently. He said that God loves us all, whatever our color and whatever our beliefs about color. This effected a positive approach, which was enhanced, in your case, by admitting the possibility that Negroes may be inferior, but that God loves them nevertheless, just as a human father loves his less intelligent children as truly as he does the genius in the family. Then by concentrating on what this implies for the church, avoiding the issue about the schools and the general social mixing of the races, he continued to strengthen your favorable attitudes."

At this point Frank broke in: "You know, Smith, you bother me. Jones has just won a major victory in persuading George to accept desegregation in the church. I'm afraid your analysis of his methods may undo his good work."

"Oh, I hope not," continued Smith. "I'm for integration. Moreover, I claim that my kind of analysis helps the non-philosopher in his practical thinking—in persuading others and in making his own decisions. Let me put it up to George. Have I undone Jones's good work or have I aided him?"

"Well, Smith, I can't say that you have done either, although you have helped clarify his effectiveness."

"I'm still uneasy," said Frank. "Perhaps it's because I've heard that Smith is an atheist and a moral skeptic."

"Your information was quite wrong, Frank. An atheist opposes a theist whereas I claim that their whole controversy is a mistake about the logic of religious terms. Expressions like 'God,' 'God loves us,' 'We are God's children,' must not be taken as referring or as trying to refer to anything; their use is partly ceremonial, being constituents in worshipful behavior, partly appraisive, persuasive, advisive, that is, practical. In the latter respect they are like 'father,' 'father loves us,' 'we are father's children' in influencing our attitudes and thereby modifying our behavior, but utterly unlike the latter in that they are not used to declare any fact.

"That goes for moral terms, too. 'We ought to treat Negroes as our brothers,' 'In the good life all men love and respect one another' do not assert a duty nor describe anything. They are injunctions to others or commitments of ourselves to do something. So far as 'reasons' are offered for them, this is not to be considered as giving evidence of their truth but as adding strength to their practical effectiveness."

At this point Frank could restrain himself no longer. "You see, George, what I mean? On Smith's account our preacher wasn't talking about God's love of all his children and the good example this sets us to love our black brothers even if we consider them inferior, nor did he lead you to think about such matters. He was simply influencing you and you were being influenced. Now, does this supposed 'insight' enhance the moving quality of his sermon?"

"Hell, no!" (I must here apologize for George's language; he was obviously upset.) "If I hadn't thought that he was talking about God and God's love and our duty to follow His example and the goodness of a certain sort of life I would not have been moved at all. I'm only a scientist, and a philosopher can get me all twisted up in semantics. But let me tell you this, Smith. When we lay-men talk about God and our moral obligations, however much we may differ in our concepts of God or the good life, we are concerned with something we take to be ob-jective, just as objective as genes or molecules—we are not simply trying to influence one another's behavior." At this point George turned and walked away without as much as a polite "Good-bye."

I want this bit of fiction to help me make my point, namely, that ordinary language is as intentional about mat-ters of value as it is about matters of fact. If it were taken somehow to prove that there is a God or that segregation is wrong because people commonly believe these things, it would thwart my purpose. A reliable determination of what is good, just as of what is the case, requires the use of methods which, though finally sanctioned by common sense, do not amount to an uncritical acceptance of some popular belief, no matter how widespread.

I think any straightforward analysis of our evaluative language must come out with the consequence that it is thoroughly objective and intentional. The proponents of the so-called emotive theory have done us both service and disservice. They are right in emphasizing that our ordinary value-talk is emotionally expressive. They are wrong when they make a sharp distinction between emotive and cogni-tive verbs and suggest that though the latter can express assertions the former cannot. If we trust ordinary speech, emotions are as assertive as any experience and as ob-jectively oriented. The whole division between emotive and cognitive terms has been foisted onto everyday language by outsiders trying to save what they can of a philosophical commitment.

Brentano, though not a linguistic analyst, had a sound sense for the vernacular in this regard. "Certain feelings," he wrote, "refer unmistakably to objects, and language itself signifies this through expressions which make use of it. We say, one is pleased with —, one is pleased about something, one grieves or sorrows over something. And again one says: that pleases me, that pains me, that makes me sad, etc. Joy and sorrow, as affirmation and denial, love and hate, desire and aversion, clearly follow a presentation and refer to what is presented in it."

Verbs descriptive of emotions do sometimes occur idiomatically in intransitive form in English, and participial adjectives are occasionally found without oblique complements, but a correct feeling for them, I think, is that in these uses they are elliptical. Besides "He's angry with her" and "I fear him" we do often say such things as "He appears to be angry" and "I tell you, I'm afraid." Still it seems relevant in the latter cases to ask, "With whom is he angry?" and "What are you afraid of?" Moreover, to make as good a case as possible for the opposition, these questions might on occasion be properly answered by "Oh, nobody in particular" or "Nothing specially." But this, I suggest, only means that in these instances the anger or fear is attached accidentally to anyone or anything that comes along, not that it completely lacks an object. I admit that there are pathological emotional states that seem quite properly described as objectless; I shall consider them later.

But now, though I agree with Brentano in insisting that *all* experience is intentional, I am uncomfortable about his sharp distinction between judgment and emotion. Just as all experience is intentional, so also it is all emotional in some degree (using "emotional" widely to include the sense of "volitional" and "appetitive"). Brentano himself uses a device, in showing that the traditional distinction between emotion and volition breaks down, which we may adopt against his division between judgment and emotion. It amounts to filling the gap between traditionally separated characterizations by intermediate ones. I realize that this can easily become a fallacy (of the form, "you cannot make any cut because any place you put it is arbitrary"), but if it is only used to give insight that the difference is one of degree, then I think it is legitimate.

Consider the sentences, "I know that she will come home" and "I long to have her come home." No one would object to classifying the main verb of the first as cognitive and that of the second as emotive. But now put between these extremes "I believe that she will come home," "I trust that she will come home," "I hope that she will come home," "I wish that she would come home." Of course we could have an oppositely toned emotive extreme, for example, "I loathe to have her come home." Here again, however, intermediaries could be found, like "I fear that she will come home," "I dislike to have her come home." Now if we concentrate on the intermediaries, such as "I trust that . . . " and "I fear that . . . ," we must admit that although they are emotive they may, in some circumstances, be only very mildly so, so mildly, indeed, that they are practically equivalent, almost losing their opposite emotive tone (of favor and disfavor), expressing little more than hesitant belief. On the other hand, if we think of the construction, "I believe that . . . ," as it actually occurs, we must admit that frequently it is not emotively neutral; it sometimes describes a favorable and sometimes an unfavorable attitude—indeed, I am willing to extend this to the form, "I know that. . . ." Imagine a man whose wife has left him for another but who still has faith that her love for him will win out. When he says, "I know that she will come home," he is clearly describing a favorable attitude toward her return. Place beside this man another who has tried to drive away his wife permanently. When he says, "I know that she will come home," he is obviously expressing an antipathy towards his wife's reappearance.

It may be objected that we can abstract from this emotive connotation of "know" and "believe" as concretely used and attend solely to their cognitive significance. But surely the same is true for the verbs "trust" and "fear" and even for "long" and "loathe." Now it may be pointed out that the last two, unlike "know," suspend the assertiveness of their subordinate clauses when used as main verbs. This brings up an important topic which will be discussed later, but for the present we need only note that this factor cannot serve to distinguish emotive from cognitive verbs. There are verbs that probably would be described as cognitive which do suspend the assertiveness of clauses subordinate to them, and others that would likely be treated as emotive which do not. An instance of the former is, "He guesses that she will come home," of the latter, "He regrets that she will come home."

Possibly the most generic emotive verb in English is "feel." This is perhaps unfortunate for our purposes, since it has so many non-emotive uses, describing touch ("The doctor felt my pulse"), functioning as a copula in certain constructions ("I feel comfortably warm"), being very nearly a synonym for "experience" ("I felt a sudden pain in my left arm"). But it does widely occur not only as an auxiliary with emotive participial adjectives ("She felt afraid of him for the first time") but as an emotive verb in its own right ("She feels her loss profoundly"). And it should be noted that in this last-mentioned usage it requires a noun or substantive clause as object or a phrase used as an oblique complement ("She feels" or even "She feels keenly and continuously" would not pass as complete sentences). Even in the auxiliary construction referred to, although no complementary phrase is demanded ("She felt very angry"), still when one is added we have the sense of an explication of meaning, not a simple increase ("She felt very angry about his leaving without an apology"). In what, then, may be characterized as its emotive occurrences, "to feel" is descriptive of an intentional experience. And it may not be without significance that it is often used in a way that is almost indistinguishable from certain admittedly cognitive verbs such as "think" or "surmise." Consider "I feel that the Supreme Court will not recess until it comes to a decision on the issue."

Cognitive and emotive uses of verbs and adjectives in English thus shade into one another so subtly and pervasively that it appears clearly improper to set up separate classes of terms descriptive of experience based on this distinction. With our approach we may treat this as evidence that experience is throughout both emotional and intentional, and that this union is not accidental.

To occur at all, it would seem that a cognition, whether perceptual or ratiocinative, must be infused with feeling of some kind and in some degree. To have the characteristic pattern of an emotion, a feeling needs to be directed, to have an object. The British empiricists were unaware of this, which no doubt is one of the reasons why their contemporary disciples have closed their eyes to so obvious a truth.

Hume tried to give a purely existential, non-intentional, account of the "passions." In his own words, "A passion is an original existence, or, if you will, modification of existence, and contains not any representative quality. . . . When I am angry, I am actually possessed with the passion, and in that emotion have no more a reference to any other object, than when I am thirsty, or sick, or more than five foot high." But though thus valiantly trying to carry through his characteristic approach to experience, his own sound sense got the better of him. Speaking of two emotions in particular, he wrote, " 'Tis evident, that pride and humility, tho' directly contrary, yet have the same *object*. This object is self." And although he went on to discuss the causes of these feelings, it is clear that when he wrote "object" he meant object. "But tho' that . . . which we call *self*, be always the object of these two passions, 'tis impossible it can be their *cause*, or be sufficient alone to excite them. For as these passions are directly contrary, and have the same object in common; were their object also their cause; it cou'd never produce any degree of the one passion, but at the same time it must excite an equal degree of the other. . . . We must, therefore, make a distinction betwixt the cause and the object of these passions; betwixt that idea, which excites them, and that to which they direct their view when excited."

In fact, it might not be amiss to point out to latter-day Humeans that Hume himself fell into intentionalistic terminology not merely about emotions but specifically about moral emotions, thus in one respect anticipating the sort of valuational empiricism to be developed later in this book. In a passage that ought to have become classic he said, "To have the sense of virtue, is nothing but to *feel* a satisfaction of a particular kind from the contemplation of a character. The very *feeling* constitutes our praise or admiration; . . . in feeling that it pleases after such a particular manner, we in effect feel that it is virtuous." Basically, what I intend to add is that our feeling that a character or action is virtuous has an inherent probability of being correct, which, of course, is modified by other relevant feelings. However, the matter is not quite as simple as this may sound, and we must immediately turn to a serious objection, namely, that there are pathological emotional states that certainly seem to be objectless and are often so described. I refer to states of general anxiety, manic euphoria, and the like.

One could counter the objection by saying that these states are not properly described as objectless, but should be characterized as having everything, or everything that comes to mind, as their objects. One could draw the analogy between the condition of general depression and the wearing of blue glasses; just as with the latter a person still sees things, and his vision does not lack objects but he sees everything as bluish, so with the former, his depression is not objectless but is about everything. However, there are those who refuse to describe in this fashion the pathological states mentioned. They say that in general anxiety, for example, one is not anxious about this, that, and whatever else one thinks of, but of nothing or in any case nothing identifiable. Let us suppose them correct. This leaves us with our problem unsolved.

One way out is to appeal to the incontrovertible fact that people generally consider these states abnormal. And what seems wrong and neurotic about them is precisely their lack of any specific objects. Why not simply say that they are not genuine emotions and thus do not fall under the generalization about all emotions being intentional? But this seems too easy an escape; it appears too much like a merely verbal way out. Moreover, the pathological states mentioned are too continuous with frequent daily experiences of a less extreme sort to be comfortably excluded from our consideration.

The solution which appears most attractive is to say that these supposedly objectless emotions do have objects but that they are hidden ones; people subject to them are self-deceived.

I imagine that this way of meeting the difficulty will be immediately challenged. First, there may be a general, a priori objection which, I think, is not too serious. How, it might be urged, can one be mistaken about one's own experiences? If one is not aware of an object of his anxiety or depression, then there is no object of these states: an outsider has no right to attribute one to them.

Our intentionalistic interpretation of experience, however, makes this line of criticism completely external and therefore irrelevant. Of course, it is logically possible to hold that any experience of physical objects may be mistaken but no consciousness of experience itself can be. Yet I can hardly conceive any empirically minded intentionalist following this path; indeed, he would seem to be pushed in the opposite direction. Experience is normally directed outwardly; if it turns inward it has as object something which itself has objects and whose characteristic nature is constituted by this fact. Hence the notorious difficulty of preserving a given experience when trying to make it the object of scrutiny. How foreign to all this is the credulous assumption that one's own experience is an open book. Historically this naïveté is easily understood. Descartes found clear and distinct ideas to be free of all possible error. Locke transferred this character to his simple ideas of sense, of which all experience is formed. It is a short step to the view that one can never be mistaken about one's own experience, even if that be a subtle compound of conflicting emotions. Whatever we may think of some of the vagaries to be found in "depth psychology," that movement should have forever put a stop to the a priorism of the line of objection we are now disallowing.

But a second type of criticism, or perhaps I had better

say "question," is not thus foreign; it merits careful consideration. It asks, "What are the hidden objects of these
apparently objectless emotions?" If no plausible answer is
forthcoming, this type of "solution" of our problem must
strike anyone as empty and unsatisfying.

By the nature of the case, my answer must be tentative,
partial and to some degree speculative. Let us concentrate
on just one of these pathological states on the supposition
that if a plausible identification of its type of hidden object
can be made, our purpose will be served, for we are interested not in surveying the details but in meeting a categorial
challenge in principle. Our method here should not be to
explore the forms of everyday speech that are descriptive
of emotions—that investigation has been made, and we
have come out with the conclusion that emotional experience is objectively oriented and where it appears to be
objectless this very fact marks it as abnormal. In trying to
align this abnormality with what we have accepted as the
characteristic form of experience, it will be necessary to use
a more empirical procedure, somewhat aided by conjecture
since "facts" are so hard to come by in this region. We
shall therefore turn to the psycho-pathologists and also to
our own observations of states which, though not psychotic,
show striking resemblances to those which are.

In Freud's early account, general anxiety was treated
as a purely physiological phenomenon, due to frustration
of the sexual orgasm. By 1923, in *The Problem of
Anxiety,* he had changed his view. He was impressed with
the similarity of anxiety to fear, which, of course, has an
object, namely, some danger, real or supposed, threatening
the ego's self-preservation. The object of fear, he now
contended, was some known, ordinarily external, danger;
that of anxiety, an unknown, internal one. The sense of
helplessness in anxiety is due to the fact that what is feared

is within one, so that one cannot escape it nor fight it in the ordinary sense, and to the fact that it is unknown, so that one cannot cope with it in any specific way. Freud, naturally, does attempt to locate it: one's instincts betray one, force the ego to commit acts making it unacceptable to the outside world or (in the mature development of the subject) to the internalized outside world, the superego.

The more recent theories of the culturally oriented analysts, such as Eric Fromm and H. S. Sullivan, are built on the position of Freud just outlined. With them, however, the threat comes not so much from biological instincts, like sex and aggressiveness, as from culturally produced pressures. One seeks social recognition yet somehow senses that this threatens the need of being considered unassuming; one desires artistic creativeness but is in a society where this, unless kept in close confines, brands one as queer, and so on.

On this account, general anxiety is to be classified as a kind of fear. Thus it has its objects, which are what is feared. They are in some sense recognized, while also in some sense not. To say that they are unconscious is misleading. It is less so to say that they are subconsciously presented, are not simply destroyed or forgotten but "repressed" or "projected." Perhaps it is best to say that the subject has a dissociated consciousness: the anxiety is a fear of something that has become separated in some queer way from recognition but not completely so, as though the fear were another person's.

My suggestion is simple and avoids taking sides in the controversy between the biologically and culturally oriented analysts (it is compatible with some combination of their views). It is that the hidden object of fear in pathological anxiety is oneself, is that at almost any moment one may do or say something that will cause one to be rejected or to lose self-respect and that adequate safeguards against this imminent danger cannot be constructed.

All this may be considered a rather large dose of theory with a comparatively small admixture of observation. But some further facts may help our case. First there are the cures that these psychoanalysts have effected—not that they themselves prove the theory correct, but the patients do come to accept their anxiety as a form of fear, of fear that they will inadvertently betray themselves, a fear whose object was, before the cure, somehow hidden or camouflaged.

Second, we can note that there are normal emotions which deceive those subjected to them about their true objects, revealing upon analysis the same mechanisms used by the psychoanalysts to explain the more severe aberrations of pathological states. Consider: "Why are you angry at me? What have I done?" Answer: "Well, to tell the truth, I'm really irritated with myself" (a case of projection). Or: "Why are you afraid of that audience? Not one of them can sing a note." Rejoinder: "Well, I guess I'm afraid of my own stage-fright—I lose breath-control" (another instance of projection). Finally: "I've felt awfully anxious about everything, even trivialities, this last week, and often quite unable to make any decision. I think I now know why—I'm fearful that I won't measure up to my new job" (an example of repression).

And this kind of deception is not confined to states universally admitted to be emotional; it can also be found in what would probably be classified as cognitive experiences. Take the statement: "I preached the virgin birth, the incarnation of the Godhead and the resurrection of the body and actually thought I believed them; now I see that what I really believed was the extraordinary spiritual greatness of Jesus' person and teachings." Now it would be rather absurd to say that in this and countless similar cases a misapprehension concerning what one believed shows that the belief had no object whatever. Indeed, there are cases of a sort of general cognitive acquiescence in which one is willing to believe whatever pops into one's head, and of its opposite in which one is skeptical about everything. We should not take these as proving that one can believe or doubt without believing or doubting anything; it would be much better to assimilate them to the sort of emotional state we have been discussing.

Third, there are cases of fear that are quite normal in the circumstances and do not involve any self-deception, yet that approach anxiety in what may be called their generalized character. I can imagine the emotional state of a much-sought criminal who has tried to hide his identity and start an honest life in some new locality. His condition must border that of one suffering pathological anxiety, since he fears that he may reveal his identity at any moment by some unguarded word or act. Only slightly removed from this unhappy state of affairs is a man whom I know rather intimately. He always undergoes panic when attending a social gathering or is required to take part in polite conversation about literature or the arts, yet he is under no misapprehension concerning the object of his fear. He has suffered all his life from one of the shortest of memories. His panic is fear that he will fail to recognize someone whom he knows well or that he will find his mind a blank about a book he read not long ago or a play he attended not more than two weeks earlier.

I trust I have shown that it is not wholly unreasonable to hold that pathological anxiety, which seems to be objectless, has hidden objects and thus fits our commonsensical view that emotional experience is intentional. And if I have, I assume that this case is sufficient to meet in principle the criticism we have been concerned with.

9

The Intentionalism of Emotional Language

UP TO THIS point we have been investigating the grammar of what I shall call "emotive" language, language that depicts emotions. Let us now turn our attention to "emotional" language, language that expresses emotions. This may prove more entertaining; it will certainly be more vulgar; however, its purpose is serious and in fact quite thoroughly academic.

Comparatively little of our ordinary speech is devoted to the description of emotions. We talk a great deal about politics and business and family affairs but not much about our emotions. On the other hand, most of our talk about these other things is emotional and indeed quite recognizably so.

But now the point I wish to make is not so much that ordinary speech is emotional as that it is emotional about other things; it commonly is not about emotions, yet it has its objects of discourse about which it speaks emotionally. "Oh, what a beautiful morning!," "Please give the blind, homeless old man a coin," "He's an ugly, disgusting monster" do not describe the speaker's emotions, but in proper context (which is not that of a book on general epistemology) they manage to express them. Moreover they put into words not merely the emotive tone of the speaker's feeling but its object as well. They are about a pleasant morning, a blind beggar, an unspecified male. I am not too unhappy about calling them "expressions" of emotion, for the very ambiguity of this term, if we take note of it, can assist our understanding of the relation between the language and the feeling.

It would be unfortunate if, realizing that sentences of the sort just illustrated are not descriptions of emotions, we were to conclude that they are merely symptoms, outward accompaniments or perhaps parts of emotions, for this would reduce them to occurrences and deny them the status of expressions in any semantic sense. But obviously they do have objects—each is about something and, indeed, the very same thing that the emotion it expresses is about (putting aside for now emotional states involving self-deception).

There are, or possibly I should say there were not long hence, those who would deny that the sentences I have mentioned are sentences at all. This denial may be legitimate relative to some ideal language these people mean to construct, but it is quite inappropriate to everyday speech or to any model adequate to it. If one were to deny that an emotionally expressive sentence is a sentence, few if any actually uttered sentences would escape condemnation.

There are others who would deny that the sentences I have used for illustration are assertive, that is, make statements. They would grant that the sentences refer, that they are about something, the very same things, in fact, that the feelings they express are about, but they would not admit that they say anything about these objects. "Obviously," these gentlemen would contend, "if the sentences you just gave said anything, they would be true or false, but your sentences are neither."

These philosophers have a point, but before attempting to locate it exactly, it might be well to have a few more sentences in mind which are unquestionably emotional but not descriptive of emotions, and to observe that they can be of any grammatical form (in the grammarian's sense of "grammatical").

First consider some examples that are declarative, and, indeed, abstracted as we must abstract them from the context of their actual use, are straightforwardly descriptive of some objective situation, their emotional expressiveness coming largely from the fact that they are uttered at all: "Your nose is running," "There's a hair in the soup you served us," "He sneezed directly in my face."

Again, take some cases that are admittedly declarative but might be classed as non-descriptive since involving a predicate noun or adjective considered not to be descriptive: "He is a lovable old rascal," "The prospect ahead was frightful," "The accident which kept me here was a very happy one." The key predicative terms in these may be thought of as "projections" of emotions, as derivatives of emotively depictive predicates now ascribed to the objects of emotions. Hence we might want to think of these cases as disguised descriptions of emotions, such as, "Everybody loves the old man though mildly disapproving his behavior," "We were frightened by the prospect ahead," "I am very happy about the accident which kept me here."

Other examples could be given of declarative yet probably non-descriptive emotional sentences which are not quite so easily interpreted as objectified emotive depictions, since their predicates are not so immediately akin to emotively descriptive adjectives. Consider a few whose crucial terms emotionally seem to derive from theological language: "She is divine, simply heavenly," "He is a goddamned liar," "Mrs. Adams is blessed indeed—with a reliable husband and well-behaved children." One can easily think of cases in which the emotionally expressive predicate is metaphorical and gets its power from association with a literal usage descriptive of situations commonly eliciting emotions of the kind expressed. "The old lady is poor indeed—she has nothing left but her money," "The weather is beastly," "The man is rotten, through and through" furnish instances.

Many emotionally expressive sentences are not declarative in form. This hardly needs illustration, but we might take a scattering sample of a variety of types. There are those that are invocative grammatically: "May God bless you" (uttered by a professional beggar), "Curses on that screw, it's fallen down the drain." Others have the form of commands: "Go jump in the lake," "Stop breathing." Then there are ostensible questions: "Who do you think you are?," "Why are you always under my feet?" Also, of course, there are exclamations: "Oh George, you're here at last!," "What a sight she is!"

Finally, let me call attention to emotional expressions which, though linguistic, are not sentences in the grammatical sense at all. There are ejaculations which are utterances of what, in sentential contexts, are perfectly good words: "Lord!," "My dear!," "Hell!" There are others which perhaps cannot properly be classified as words at all, but are clearly conventional, differing from one vernacular to another: in English, for example, we have the interjections "pshaw," "whew," "ouch," "ah."

It is beyond debate that in these last instances we have expressions of emotions that describe nothing and cannot properly be classified as true or false. And we must agree that the very first ones (despite their declarative form) and all the other types sampled are non-descriptive in their function of being emotionally expressive. For example, "Your nose is running" is descriptive and true or false so far as assertive of the fact that your nose is running. Its emotional expressiveness arises from its being uttered at all —addressed, say, not to one's three-year-old but to one's wife in the course of a heated argument. As thus expressive it is neither true nor false, not being assertive of any fact.

But having gone this far with our critics, we should call a halt. To begin with, we should emphasize what they admit, that all these utterances precisely in their emotional expressiveness have objects, namely, the very objects of the feelings they express. Moreover, we should point out that the expressions mentioned say, in a perfectly good sense of "say," something about their objects, and, so far as they are successful as emotional expressions, they say exactly what the emotions they express say.

In making this out, I suppose the last group to which I referred presents more difficulties than the first. If we can succeed here we should be able to do so with the others. First we note that these interjections have objects. What they are must ordinarily be determined within the context of their concrete occurrence, but sometimes further words in conventional language help identify them: "Ah, that news relieves my fears," "Brrr! It's cold in here." And when these further words are missing, such a question as, "What are you 'oh'-ing and 'ah'-ing about?" is often entirely relevant. But now about what they say. Consider these cases: (1) "Pshaw! I just missed my train," (2) "Whew! an inch closer and that taxi would have struck me," (3) "Ouch! that stove's hot." "Pshaw," "whew" and "ouch" in these expressions are not merely directed toward things and events; they succeed in putting into words the emotions they express. Suppose we had, (1a) "Pshaw, I just caught my train," (2a) "Whew! an inch to one side and that taxi would not have struck me," (3a) "Ouch! that stove is pleasantly warm." This last set would all be misuses of the interjections, whereas the first would be quite appropriate.

Now it might be contended that this difference merely marks what are the conventions in American speech. This could, of course, be the case if, for example, someone unacquainted with our habits uttered (1a), (2a) or (3a). But now suppose that this is not the case, that it is a native American who utters these sentences and uses the interjections in them to express just what is ordinarily expressed by them. Then we would wonder at the odd feelings he has in these situations; it would be almost like seeing a father smile in amusement when recognizing that the drowned boy is his only child. We would think, "Perhaps the man secretly wanted to stay home, and so felt as he did when he said 'pshaw' about catching his train" or "That fellow must be one of the gang that deliberately throw themselves in the path of taxis in order to collect damages, so that 'whew' expressed his relief at how close he had come to having his plans go awry."

I give you these speculations to indicate how the interjections in (1a), (2a) and (3a) may be inappropriate in two quite different ways, first in that they are not the correct conventional sounds to express the feelings involved, second in that these feelings are queer and unfitting under the circumstances. In both these misuses they resemble descriptive terms, which may err by not fitting the linguistic conventions or by expressing a belief which is wrong.

My point is that emotionally expressive language, taken precisely in its expressiveness, says something about an object; what it manages to convey in conventional terms, supposing that it is expressive, is something said by the feeling it expresses. It is properly described, therefore, as a translation (however partial and inadequate) of that feeling. It does not simply give vent to the latter, it puts it into conventional language; it is not merely an effect, it is a surrogate. In this respect, then, it acts as a proxy, and I have debated using this term for it. I have decided against this designation for two reasons. First, for convenience, there is the value of keeping emotionally expressive sentences distinct from proxies for perceptions without too much semantical jargon. Second, emotionally expressive language does not occur simply as a translation of the feelings expressed by it. Its relations to the latter are complex and I would like to keep this before us also.

A proxy forms no part of its original; it simply stands in place of it, saying (in part) what it says. Expressions of emotion frequently themselves add color to and enrich the feelings they express. The "general semanticists," for all their excesses, do make the perfectly good point that we often talk ourselves into emotional states. For our present purposes, this is a bad way to put it since it is essentially causal. It does suggest the semantical truth, however, that emotions talk about their objects to a very great degree through conventional, though in many cases inaudible, language. Think how emotionally pallid one's life would be, emptied of all the curses, invocations, self-accusations, commands, questions, interjections requiring the vernacular of one's native tongue. Although much would happen (how much it is perhaps impossible to tell) to one's perceptual experience if one could get it purified of conventional terms, it would still be, I surmise, less completely washed out.

Then, too, emotionally expressive language has a strong tendency to reinstate an emotion if the emotion has lapsed or to aggravate it if it is still present. This is close to the quality just noted and may be a consequence of a process sometimes called "redintegration," that is, the reinstitution of a total mental state by the recurrence of a part of the experience of something similar to a part. This again has been stated causally but may have some bearing on the intentional character of our emotions and certainly marks off their expressions from perceptual proxies which, though they may stimulate imagination, hardly reinstitute perceptions like their originals.

These differences seem to mark off expressions of emotions as more closely connected with the occurrence and, so to speak, the very being, the nature of, the feelings expressed than proxies are to their perceptual originals. It would follow that it should be more difficult to distinguish sharply between expressions of emotions and descriptions of them than between perception-proxies and perception-depicters. And this appears to me to be so. It seems improper to draw any very heavy line between the pair "Would that he were coming" and "I wish that he were coming," but we quite readily separate "He is coming" and "I see him coming."

Then, too, expressions of emotion seem more intimately bound up with the personality of the speaker, with his experience as characteristically *his,* than are perception-proxies. This no doubt reflects a difference in what these sentences translate—our emotions are more genuinely part of us than our perceptions.

Moreover, as we have noted, sentences of any grammatical form can function as expressions of feelings, but only declarative sentences can properly translate perceptions. This is of course a major distinction. It may make one hesitate to characterize emotional expressions as "translations," although it should not; certainly it is no more difficult, in general, to translate a question or command from one conventional language to another than a declaration.

"But do non-declarative sentences say anything?" I

shall be asked. Obviously they do not describe any fact. I think it best to admit that they do not declare anything. But they can evaluate, not always judiciously and after deliberation, but in many cases, I think, unmistakably. And this is quite properly expressed as a way of "saying" something. If we think back about the instances of emotionally expressive language given earlier, we must admit that at least most of them are directed toward their objects as something good or bad, to be accepted or rejected, to be done or not done, and so forth. This aspect will be developed and analyzed in later chapters.

Let me summarize the present chapter. Our emotionally expressive language in everyday life does not ordinarily describe our emotions; it expresses them. This does not simply mean that it is caused by them, is a symptom of them, perhaps forms part of them (although all this may be involved); it means that such language translates them into conventional terms, evaluating their objects as emotions themselves do.

This way of speaking presupposes the legitimacy of thinking of emotions as themselves linguistic, as having objects in a semantical sense and saying something about them (in a non-declarative, evaluative manner). It should be noted that this is in accord with the intentionalistic interpretation of experience in general that constitutes the categorial framework of our whole approach.

But now we must note an anomaly. I have said that all or certainly almost all of our everyday talk is emotionally expressive. This implies that many of our perception-proxies, perception-depicters and descriptions of emotions are emotionally expressive. Yet I have tried to distinguish expressions of emotions from descriptions of them and from translations and depictions of our perceptions. Does this not involve a contradiction?

It would if I had meant by "expressions of emotion" a special class of sentences or other linguistic elements to be separated from the other sentences mentioned. Let me now clarify myself. I have in mind, by this term, any bits of conventional speech taken as performing a certain function. "I hate you, I hate you, I hate you" does, I suppose, describe in some rather undiscriminating way the speaker's feelings, but it certainly also expresses them. An inadvertent eavesdropper might remark, "I take it she hates him." This would describe the same emotion but not express it.

My classification therefore is mixed. When our ordinary language is ideally clarified, perception-proxies, perception-depicters and descriptions of emotions are linguistic elements (sentences) forming mutually exclusive classes; expressions of emotion are functions that any linguistic elements or certainly any sentences can perform. This, too, will demand further analysis, but I think it does not introduce any contradiction. When I distinguish between, let us say, a proxy for a perception and an expression of an emotion, I have in mind a functional difference which, in a given instance, may appear in two different sentences but need not.

10

The Syntax of Emotions

I PROPOSE to treat emotions as sentences. My main purpose in so speaking of them is to emphasize their intentional character. Moreover, by calling them "sentences" rather than "words" or, more loosely, "symbols," I want to specify that they make a kind of claim, that they "say" something. This something, as already hinted, is a value sort of thing. It is upon emotions that I shall base our comprehension of values just as I used perceptions as the foundation of our knowledge of facts.

But now if it seemed a little awkward to talk about perceptions as true or false, certainly it must appear completely inappropriate to speak of emotions in this way. I agree; hence I propose to characterize them not as true or false but as legitimate or illegitimate. This may seem at first simply a verbal dodge. It is, I believe, something more substantial. It involves the kind of claim our feelings make. This should become clear as we analyze the grammar of emotions and investigate its semantical significance. It is best, I think, to approach our task obliquely, through a consideration of conventional sentences connected with emotions.

We have distinguished two main types of such sentences, those that express and those that depict emotions. Let us begin by noting some peculiarities of the former. Although any sentence can (and I am inclined to think that every sentence does) express an emotion, it will be most suitable to our present purpose to start with declarative ones.

Some years ago my wife had promised our three sons a pleasant surprise. The morning of its disclosure arrived, and upon its presentation all three exclaimed, "It's a kitten!" Taken as a statement of fact, the sentence was true or false, but as so taken it was not an expression of emotion. Actually the youngest uttered it with rising inflection, the oldest with falling voice and the middle in a matter-of-fact tone. It was easy to see that the youngest was delighted, the oldest disappointed and the middle unmoved by the gift. Considered as expressions of these emotions, the three utterances made a sort of claim, that their mother's present was good, was bad, was so-so (to put it very roughly). To say this, is not to deny that the exclamations performed other functions as well: they no doubt relieved emotional tensions, communicated socially, guided future decisions (the oldest boy had wanted a puppy) and so on. But doing these other things did not prevent their making the sort of claim indicated; indeed some of these other functions rested squarely upon the presence in them of such a claim.

For example, guidance of his mother's future choices was offered by the oldest son precisely because the expression of his disappointment managed to say (as the feeling it expressed said) that the gift was inappropriate.

Let us attend, for a moment, to the reactions of the youngest and the oldest. As descriptions of fact, they agreed; as expressions of emotions, they disagreed. It has become popular of late, particularly in American philosophical circles, to treat this latter disagreement as simply a factual matter, not, that is, as a disagreement about fact, but one of fact. But how facts, whether physical or mental, can disagree is something I cannot understand: they simply occur; it is claims about them that can disagree (and through metaphor, people who make them).

I may describe the emotions of the two boys as one of delight and another of disappointment about the kitten, but in this of course there is no disagreement, for the facts here described are different ones. Nevertheless, as descriptions, these statements clearly present claims. As expressions of emotions, it may be thought that they do not. However, the two utterances can disagree only because, having the same object (namely, the gift of the kitten), they make in some sense rival claims about it. If we deny this element of claim, wherein is the conflict between them? Surely there is none in the mere difference of intonation, one rising and the other falling. Nor in the ramifications of the emotional expressions taken as facts—the frown of the older boy, the smile of the younger, and so on.

It may be suggested that the opposition lies in the further actions which tend to follow these emotional expressions, but this simply places the same problem in another location. Different actions as actually occurring do not disagree; they merely differ. Suppose one son left the room, the other stayed to fondle the kitten; in these facts there is still no opposition. Of course, if one had tried to remove the animal and the other to retain it, there would have been conflict. But note that in this case there would have been incompatible objectives, one boy attempting to bring about exactly what the other opposed; both could not have succeeded. One would have aimed at a fact which the other wanted to prevent. Here we have an instance of disagreement, but in what does it consist? Not in any fact—not, say, in the removal of the cat or even in blows struck (our sons frequently boxed and tussled good-naturedly, that is, without disagreement)—but in some contrariety of claim about a fact or possible fact, namely,

the kitten's eviction. Not, of course, in a statement or prediction of the fact (disinterested observers of the conflict
might have disagreed on its outcome, but this would have
been a different opposition). The disaccord here is not
about what will be but what shall be. We have thus a
rivalry of claims about a fact, but not about whether it is or
will be a fact. They are in some way more complex claims,
claims embracing the fitness, the desirability of a (possible)
fact.

This sort of outcome should lead us to the recognition
that in the emotional expressions with which we started,
particularly when one admits that they were in disagreement, there is an element of claim; they "say" something,
but not a factual something. Yet it relates to a fact (in
our instance, that the surprise is a kitten); it is a more
complex claim—a value claim about the fact, not a declaration of the fact. It is no distortion of everyday usage to
say that the expression of delight with the gift is favorable
to it, that of disappointment unfavorable. And this, it
seems to me, marks a general pattern.

All sentences that express emotions have what I shall
call a "factual content." When they are not declarative in
form, they do not explicitly, or even in many cases im-
plicitly, declare this content to be fact; yet the content is
factual because it could significantly be affirmed as fact,
and it is in this character that it enters the emotional expression. In some types of non-declarative expressions of
emotion the factual content emerges quite clearly. In an
imperative it is usually what is commanded. If I tell you
to walk quietly, it is that you walk quietly. In an emotionally expressive question it is often the subject of the
question. If I ask you who you think you are, it is that
you think you are somebody (of importance). With other
varieties of emotional sentences it is sometimes difficult to

make the factual content out from the words alone. Often a sympathetic reconstruction of the accompanying behavior and situation of the speaker is required. It is, roughly, that about which one is expressing himself emotionally. If it is (as it sometimes is) or were (in cases where it is not) declared as fact, the expression would in this regard be true or false. But as so considered the emotional factor is omitted. As emotionally expressive the utterance can run the gamut between the extremes of high favor and excessive disfavor, including a neutral region of indifference. If I err here, as I think I do, it is in the direction of oversimplification. Let me speak as though we had just three values of this emotional claim: for, against and indifferent towards the factual content involved, that is, not towards an affirmation of fact, but towards the fact, if it is a fact, or towards its being a fact, if it were to be one. Recall the three boys and the kitten.

The pattern of emotional expressions I have tried to point out is one of a sort of claim, to be distinguished from a factual assertion and yet not unrelated to the latter. Suppose, in any given instance, we were to substitute for the factual content its negative correlate. This would clearly have a bearing upon the emotional claim. If you replaced "It's a kitten!" by "It's not a kitten!" you could not preserve the youngest son's rising inflection and pretend to retain the same emotional claim. Nor could you do so by reversing that claim, so to speak, from favor to disfavor as though you had a double negative that canceled out. The middle son might well continue his indifference whether convinced that the gift was or was not a kitten, and the eldest would not need, in the interest of emotional consistency, to be favorably inclined to its not being a kitten (what he wanted was a puppy, not the absence of a kitten). So we must not think of the emotional claim as a sort of truth-function of the factual content (or of the truth-claim of that content if it were to be made into a declarative); yet, as I have just pointed out, it is not unrelated to that content.

If we turn from sentences taken as expressing emotions to statements that depict them we may gain further light on the pattern of the claim embedded in the feelings themselves. Hazardous as it is, the job of filling in the gaps of idiomatic speech must be undertaken before we can attain the right overlook. Not only is it elliptical to say "John is angry," it is similarly so if one says "John is angry with Mary." To get the whole picture we must have something like "John is angry with Mary for not singing as the rules require."

Against this it may be objected that simple statements of emotion often appear final and without need of expansion. Consider "John loves Mary." For ordinary speech this seems eminently adequate as a description of John's emotion, particularly if it is a case of puppy love. It would seem irrelevant and (to John) impertinent to ask, "What is it about Mary that John loves?" Of course it just might be permissible to answer that he adores everything about her, and if so the question would be legitimate. Moreover, if John impulsively or through necessity were to marry Mary, he might, when in later life condemned for not loving his wife, justify himself by saying "My wife is not the Mary I loved as a youngster; she has changed, has lost her winsome characteristics and developed some very unattractive ones." If this line is to be open to John in the future he must admit now, as a youth, that he doesn't love a bare individual but one appropriately endowed with properties. I am inclined to hold that it is persons, not particulars abstracted from their attributes, that people cherish or despise.

Very well. What must we do to square everyday expressions with this? "John loves Mary" would then need to be interpreted as elliptical. What John loves is Mary's having a pair of blue eyes, a dimple in her right cheek, a way of turning suddenly pensive in the midst of a playful mood, a . . . , a . . . , etc. No one of these characterizations is sufficient (unless John is a very, very simple boy); it is only the ensemble that is the object of his passion. It would follow that when John tells Mary, "I love you," he is saying something very complex, indeed. But I wonder if this isn't actually so?

I am suggesting that we clarify everyday speech, idealize it, if you please. There would then be a rule to the effect that a complete description of an emotion must, besides the emotive verb, contain a secondary one subordinate to it, either in an oblique participial phrase or in a substantive clause in the accusative.

We may say of such sentences that they are complex, not that they are compound. Although they contain two verbs, they do not make two independent assertions; indeed, I am inclined to think they make only one, but if they sometimes do make two, one is always subordinate to the other, involving a specification of it through a designation of its object. They are like "He shouted to us that he was inside," not "He was inside and shouted to us." He hoped that she would come" obviously cannot be analyzed into the double affirmation—of his hoping and her future coming; but neither can reference to her coming be omitted. It might at first thought appear attractive to treat "that she would come" as a name—this would avoid making it an assertion while still allowing it meaning, which of course must be retained. But what would it name? Clearly not itself, for the whole sentence does not describe his feelings towards these or any other words. The only answer having any plausibility whatever is that it designates the fact that she will come. But then if there is no such fact, the clause does not name anything and so, on this interpretation, is completely meaningless. The consequence is that, if she has not or does not come, "He hoped that she would come" is reduced in significance to "He hoped." This of course is absurd.

Not all descriptions of emotions suspend the assertion of fact in their subordinate clauses. "He was angry that she had come" does not. Yet it is important to see that here too we have a complex, not a compound, sentence. The case just given is quite different from "She had come and he was angry," for it tells us what he was angry about. So here, although a fact is declared, its mode of declaration shows us something about the emotion being depicted. It shows us that the emotion is complex and in essentially the same way as in the other case, namely, "He hoped that she would come," in which the factual claim of the subordinate clause is suspended. Indeed, to bring this out I would like to propose that we think of "He was angry that she had come" as suspending the factual assertion mentioned just in so far as it is depictive of the emotion and consider that its declaration of this fact shows that it performs another job as well.

But now, although depictions of emotions suspend, in some cases at least, the factual claim in their subordinate clauses, they do so because they describe the emotions; the emotions are their objects, so that we must not suppose that their semantical relation to the objects of the emotions is just the same as that of the emotions themselves. I do find that some emotions suspend the assertiveness of their reference to fact, and this seems to me to reveal something vital about all emotions. But it is not the same suspension as that found in their depicters, since, as I have said, the latter is the result of the intention introduced by description—the depicter, if adequate, specifies the object of the emotion in order to characterize the emotion, not to make any other claim about it and obviously not to declare it as fact. As a description of his anger, "He was angry with her for coming" does need to refer to the purported fact, that she had come, but *in this capacity* it does not (if one agrees to follow my proposal) assert it. Here again we have some tidying up of colloquial speech, but this seems necessary. If we were to say "He was angry over the idea of her coming" we would have changed the obvious meaning of the original, which does not have any of his ideas as the object of his feeling. One could say, "He was angry over the supposed fact of her coming," but this idiomatically would commit one to the falsity of the belief that she has come, and we want to describe the emotion without such further involvement in factual matters. So, as I have suggested, we can have the depicter suspend the assertion in the subordinate clause. On the other hand, I think we should admit that the anger does not suspend it, and in this regard anger is to be contrasted with hope, for his hope that she would come does not involve an affirmation that she will.

To bring out the difference in these two suspensions of the assertion in reference to fact, let us bring in a third one. Statements of indirect discourse are complex, not compound, including a subordinate clause whose claim is suspended. Take as an example, "Khrushchev said that Russia will overtake America in per capita income." This sentence purports to describe a past event, but it is, in a way, a peculiar one. It is a linguistic occurrence considered not as a physical event with physical properties (the sounds he made, for example, as he uttered certain Russian words) but as intentional. Now the intention of Khrushchev's statement was assertive, claiming a future fact.   Our report of it, in indirect discourse, means to convey this without commitment to it.   We have here, so to speak, an intention within an intention.   The contained intention is only intended, so, although it is itself an assertion, it is not asserted.   The whole report would break down if it were omitted, becoming "Khrushchev said." On the other hand, we would change its character entirely if we tried to name the fact he affirmed (suppose we designate it "operation x," making our report, "Khrushchev spoke of operation x"), for then our report would have to admit the fact and omit the affirmation.   No, our statement in indirect discourse must retain the element of declaration of fact while yet suspending it; this it does by referring to it.

This suspension is very much like that which occurs in the complex sentences descriptive of emotions.   Indeed, if I am justified in treating emotions as themselves sentences in the natural language of our immediate experience, it is the same.   But waiving this contention for the moment, we can still say that indirect discourse and depiction of emotion are alike because their suspension of the claim embodied in their subordinate clauses is due to the fact that they are not themselves making it but only referring to it (reporting it in the one case and including it as a specifying element in a total description in the other).

Now this suspension, though like that frequently found in our emotions themselves, cannot be identified with the latter.   I can equally describe a man's hope that something may occur or his anger that something has taken place, and in both descriptions I can hold at arm's length any declaration that these events will happen or have happened.   But the anger itself may embody a claim of occurrence of its object that is somehow suspended in hope's comparable reference.   The suspension when it occurs must be of a different kind, springing from a different source.   I believe

it reflects the emotion's evaluative function.   It favors or
disfavors something.   What?   Some fact or possible fact,
something consequently to be referred to by a clause or
verbal phrase.   But the favoring or disfavoring, the evaluating, is not itself a declaration of the fact which is its
object.   So the fact is intended but not declared, for the intention of it is included in another, the evaluating.   Hence
the suspension.   But note: the reference to the fact is not
the object of another intention, as it is in indirect discourse.
We report Khrushchev's claim and thereby remove ourselves from that claim.   But a man, in hoping that some
woman will come, does not hope for some claim of her
coming but for the fact of her coming itself.   Yet he does
so without declaring this fact.

And this gives us some insight into emotion generally.
Although ordinarily when one is angry one's anger affirms
its object to be a fact, this is not integral to it as evaluative,
as unfavorable.   Just as a man may hope for a woman's
arrival, so also he may dread it, and in neither case does his
feeling declare it.   We may then say, I think, that all emotions are directed toward facts without, *so far as* they are
evaluative of them, declaring them.

Expressions of emotions and depictions of them both
indicate the peculiar complexity of the intention to be found
in emotions themselves.   Adequate descriptions ideally take
the form of complex sentences, the main verb referring to
the emotion, the subordinate clause or verbal phrase to its
object as something integral to it.   Expressions of emotion
embrace a factual content which may or may not be declared, but as expressive they translate into conventional
speech the flavor of the emotion as directed towards the fact
which this content does or could declare.   The emotive depicter is best in showing the structure of feeling; it is misleading since, as descriptive, its own assertion is factual and

true or false. The emotional expression is most helpful in indicating the non-factual claim that emotions make; it may take one astray by not pointing up the intentional character of feelings. By putting both together we can get some assistance in understanding the kind of intentionality characteristic of emotions themselves.

Brentano, trusting common speech as corroborative of his own phenomenological analysis, had the valid insight that emotions are intentional. Had he analyzed the grammar of ordinary language further, he should have seen the peculiar complexity of that intention (we find hints that he had glimpsed this, but they are not systematically followed up[1]). This would have run counter to his tendency to treat loving and hating as simple mental acts. Feelings not merely have objects; they have objects which in some queer way involve facts, facts that are or could in the last analysis be perceived if they do or were to exist.

One might try to state this by saying that emotions are composed of perceptions (using "perceptions" in the broad sense we have given it to include anticipations and memories when in the non-conventional language of immediate experience). This would be inappropriate, however, on at least two grounds. First, perceptions, as such, lack the warmth, the distinctive flavor of emotions, and no mere collection or grouping of them would seem sufficient to supply this deficiency. Second, emotions seem to involve our whole mental existence when they occur in a way in which perceptions do not; when we're angry, we're angry "clear through" but we can perceive several things at once.

1. He wrote: "It is certainly not necessary that anyone who loves something should think that it exists, or even only might exist; nevertheless every love is a love that something should exist. . . . So it seems to be a matter of fact unthinkable, that a being should be endowed with the faculty of love and hate, without partaking of that of judgment."

This last difference could be handled by classifying perceptions as abstractions from emotional states considered as concrete occurrences. This is attractive and we should not flatly exclude it as a possibility, but it has certain consequences we ought to avoid. The chief one is that it presents the mind-body problem in an almost unmanageable form, for it gives us mental existents as well as physical and thus introduces the nasty problem of their causal interactions. I have already suggested an escape from this by confining events to physical happenings, some of which (certain neural ones) have an intentional dimension. We could now add to this that when we loosely speak of a total mental event or state, such as is involved in an emotional experience, what we correctly refer to is a total cerebral event with all its intentional complexity, from which perceptions can be considered as abstractions.

This is attractive and I do not immediately see any fatal weakness in it. One objection that might be offered against it is that the hypothalamus seems to be the "seat" of the emotions, whereas perceptions must be "placed" in certain higher centers of the cerebrum. Walter B. Cannon has urged this against the Jamesian theory of emotions. I am, of course, in no position to judge the merits of this contention. I understand that experts do not agree that Cannon's case has been conclusively established. It would be easy to say that the issue is physiological and so does not concern us; we would need only to extend neural events to include those in the hypothalamus. This is no doubt strictly true, but there are filaments, weaker than logical implications yet not to be broken carelessly, that must be considered. It was quite natural for Cannon to move from his physiological investigations to the phenomenological speculation that there is a special emotional quality added by the hypothalamus to any perceptual elements involved in our motor-affective states. On the other hand, any physi-ological consequences of James's theory arose from his analysis of emotion into a confused consciousness of bodily changes following directly upon the perception of the ex-citing fact. For James the special flavor of any emotion was to be found in the confused perception of bodily changes it involved. I think we could square our intention-al analysis of emotion with either of these accounts, but it seems to fit the Jamesian theory much more readily, and I shall devote a few words to pointing this up.

James identified emotion with the experience of bodily reverberation, set up by the perception of the exciting fact. This is the lead we want to follow, but it does not immedi-ately appear to go in the right direction. Our reliance upon common speech and thought has gained for us the insight that feelings are intentional but not that they are exclusive-ly directed upon bodily changes. I may of course fear a pain I experience in the region of my heart and I sometimes am irritated with a headache, but it would be quite wrong to describe the emotion I have when a vicious dog unex-pectedly lunges at me as a fear of my visceral changes or a spat with my wife as an irritation with my muscular tensions. Even in the cases in which the exciting object is an event in one's own body, it is not the perception of it which, on James's theory, constitutes one's feelings, but the experience of somatic reverberations it calls forth.

Nevertheless, by a modification which seems to me to be in the spirit, if not the letter, of James, we can bring his analysis into agreement with common conceptions. What needs to be done is to draw the perception of the exciting object into the emotion itself and to have it determine the direction of the total emotive state. This is not to destroy the somatic factor; it is our confused perception of the bodily repercussions of the experience of the exciting object which gives the whole its emotional tone. But, to borrow a phrase from Knight Dunlap, the somatic perception enters the emotion as its "dynamic background."

Semantically stated, a total emotion is complex; it refers to bodily changes and to an exciting object (usually an external event). But it is not compound; the latter reference determines the intention of the whole, the former qualifies this as something different from a factual assertion, a bare perception (or memory or anticipation), marking it as emotional, as favorable, unfavorable or indifferent.

This approach explains the intimately personal character of emotions lacking in perceptions (taken as such). In popular judgment I am held responsible for my emotions to a greater degree than for my perceptions (save as the latter themselves reveal emotional tendencies, as in the case of Peeping Toms); my emotional patterns are taken to define my personality; profound changes in them or dissociations of them are deep threats to my personality. Put psychologically, the self enters experience through the somatic component of emotions. Something similar can be said when our interest is epistemological. Our favoring and disfavoring evaluations of actual or possible facts are taken to be more personal (and thus more suspect) than our perceptual affirmations of fact. This of course raises the issue whether we can ever properly claim "knowledge" of value, but for the moment I am simply pointing out that our account has a place for the greater hesitancy to admit emotional knowledge of value than perceptual knowledge of fact.

But I sense an antipathy to this analysis, particularly on the part of those who may be under the influence of Teutonic romanticism or Gallic existentialism. "Are you not bidding us essentially to accept American behaviorism with its denial of the self and everything spiritual?" I may be asked. As thus plainly and directly put, the question can be answered with a simple "No." The self is not the body nor are emotions changes in it. There is a spiritual (or as I would prefer to call it, a "mental") character here; it is that of experience itself, which is irreducibly intentional whereas nothing physical is. I have been speaking all along (as was James) of experiences of the body and its modifications; the latter, in the picture of emotions being sketched, appear as objects, not as existents.

If it be asked, "What sort of being has these experiences?," then, to follow out a hint dropped earlier, I would need to reply, "One's body, or specifically, certain neural events in it"—or in any case, its "having," as a semantical dimension, the intentions mentioned would come the closest of anything within my framework to the "having" of an experience called for by the questioner. Nor would I be too disconcerted if it were pointed out that I used a possessive personal pronoun, "one's" body, quite in line with ordinary speech, "my" body, "yours," "his," and so on. For we equally speak of "one's" mind, or spirit or soul or even self. I am not at all sure what the use of the possessive implies in these cases (except that it is *not* ownership in any property-sense), but it clearly does not disappear any more readily in spiritualistic than in physicalistic language—indeed, I can much more easily identify "my" body by observable, empirical properties than I can "my" soul or spiritual self. And ordinary language is surely not unequivocally in favor of a spiritualistic terminology; witness "I cut myself," "I locked myself in," "She destroyed herself, by throwing herself before an oncoming train."

But all of this leads into ontological disputation which I beg leave to avoid, as far as possible, in the context of this inquiry. However, it is relevant to spend a few minutes trying to meet another objection arising from quite a different systematic orientation, particularly since it is semantical and its answer will help us with our analysis. "Professor Hall," I may be asked, "have you not committed a form of the pathetic fallacy, ascribing to external things (as the objects of the total emotion) properties which really are confused perceptions of somatic changes?"

First, let us bear in mind that in daily speech there is ever present a strong tendency to commit just this fallacy, to speak not of one's horror but of the horrible accident, not of one's pleasure but of the pleasant luncheon. On the account given above, this propensity is easily understood. The dynamic background is, abstractly considered, a confused perception of bodily changes, but concretely it is a background in the total emotion, and that, as a whole, has the exciting (usually external) event as its object. Here our metaphor of emotion, in its intentional character, as a complex sentence may assist. One can think of each of the two verbs in such a sentence as making its assertion; so with emotion, which one can see as composed of two sets of perceptions—of the bodily agitation and of the exciting object. But this way of viewing it omits its distinctive character. In the conventional complex sentence, the subordinate clause makes more specific the assertion in the main verb by indicating its object (in indirect discourse, for example, it tells us what was said); it thus acts grammatically as the object in the whole sentence. So in an emotion, the perception of the exciting fact centers and gives intentional direction to the whole, but not by destroying the somatic factor or somehow just adding the predications in the latter to its own, as though the object of the whole underwent the visceral and muscular processes confusedly perceived in the body. In general, our bodily reactions to events affecting us emotionally are for, against or indifferent to them. It is this, I suggest, that is taken over from our experience of them viewed abstractly and orients it to the object of the whole emotion when considered concretely as forming the dynamic background of the latter. The body, so to speak, is felt to favor, disfavor or be neutral towards the object experienced emotionally.

I shall attempt to carry this analysis of the semantics of emotion somewhat further in the next chapter, especially as regards its three-valued character and the bearing of this upon our value judgments. But there is an objection that should be considered here.

It will be remembered that I criticized any sharp distinction between cognitive and emotive verbs and thus, by implication, between the mental states or intentions they depict. But now if we treat emotions as three-valued, it would seem that we should mark them off clearly from cognitions. We can say that he desired her coming, dreaded it or felt indifferent about it; on the other hand, we properly speak of his believing or disbelieving that she would come. However, we are permitted by everyday usage to say that he hadn't made up his mind or again that he had no belief about it one way or the other. In one sense this furnishes a strict parallel between feeling and belief, in another not. There are cases in which a man is unsettled in his belief, is at odds with himself, now believing something and now disbelieving it. These correspond to emotional conflicts, when one is torn between love and hate of the same person. Besides these there are instances of genuine suspension of judgment. These are like states of emotional indifference.

Still there is an important dissimilarity. This is brought forcibly to our attention by the undeniable fact that we may either believe or disbelieve something towards which we have a favorable feeling, for example, an increase in salary which, according to rumor, is coming our way; or again, we may believe or disbelieve something we strongly disfavor, say the nomination of a segregationist governor of the state. These are not cases of emotions felt toward other emotions, for the feeling and the belief is in each instance directed toward the same object. Nor are they cases of conflicts of emotions, as would be presented by a state of mind both favoring and disfavoring the same thing.

My suggestion is that we interpret cognitive verbs, such as "believe," as referring more abstractly to a total experience than do emotive verbs. What is omitted by the former is precisely the character of favorableness or unfavorableness. Let us recall that "emotion" is used broadly to include what used to be called "volition." (The barbarous expression, "motor-affective state," would be a less misleading term, but it is just too horrible to use at all frequently.) States of will, resolve, decision, purpose have, I think, the same general pattern as those of emotion, save that, perhaps, the general tonus of the skeletal musculature plays a more dominant role in the dynamic background, visceral and autonomic components being more pronounced in what we would commonly designate "an emotion." Moreover, the perception of the exciting object has always in it an element of anticipation in volition, thus giving the whole experience an orientation towards the future less characteristic of emotions and sometimes absent from them altogether.

Now, belief enters this picture in association with our volitional mental states and precisely with their distinctively volitional character. Let us think of it as a volitional state considered abstractly or under a certain aspect, namely when the somatic factor in the experience is treated simply as a perception of the body's readiness to act, ignoring the character of that action, that is, ignoring whether it be favorable, unfavorable or neutral toward the object of the whole state. Disbelief, as contrasted with the absence of belief, can be found in our experience of inhibited tendencies to act. This of course makes disbelief more complex, psychologically, than belief, which is perhaps borne out to some degree by the fact that belief seems to be a more normal and primitive attitude than disbelief. If our total mental state at any one time has the design of an emotion, that is, is intentional in the complex way outlined earlier, his has the consequence that all states of consciousness are specimens, however mild, of belief or its opposite. I think I personally would not be unhappy with this outcome.

Something, however, must be done about those cases in which we believe something but are not inclined to do anything about it. I propose that we take care of these by widening the sense of "doing something" about their objects. First, let us make it include readinesses to react either favorably or unfavorably as the situation develops. Suppose I see a strange dog but feel no impulse either to run from him or to make friends with him. Yet if I am aware of him and believe that he is there, I am not taken quite as much by surprise if he lunges at me or leaps playfully in my path as I would have been if I had not seen him and had no belief about his presence. Now this, I suggest, involves a kind of readiness for any of several lines of behavior which in some subtle way is perceived and forms a background to the perception of the dog so that I may properly be said to believe in his proximity.

Second, let us broaden the meaning of our phrase to cover readiness to act verbally, to talk about the object in certain ways, for example, to affirm its existence. This extension is especially useful in taking care of beliefs in past events. It calls for two additional remarks. I have, for simplicity's sake, adopted James's terminology and spoken of the "perception" of the exciting object, only warning that this phraseology is not to exclude anticipation and memory. I would now like to add that conventional language may carry the intention of the emotional or volitional state as a whole. The telegram that my son has been injured may be the only "vehicle" bearing the objective reference toward which my emotional concern and my volitional decision to see him are directed: I need not "picture" his injury in order to have strong feelings about it. Likewise, the somatic component of emotional and volitional states may be largely composed of perceptions of subvocal utterances or readinesses to talk in certain ways. Putting these together we get the conclusion, which seems to me quite agreeable with the facts, that we have emotional and volitional experiences almost wholly "composed" of talk. Our stream-of-consciousness writers, such as James Joyce, seem to bear me out in this, but any academic man, especially in such a predominantly verbal undertaking as philosophy, can hardly fail to concur.

Similarly in simplicity's sake I have largely fallen into an episodic rather than a dispositional way of talking about emotive and cognitive matters. I have argued elsewhere,[2] and shall not repeat it here, that both episodic and dispositional terms are appropriate to characterize mental subject matter, as also to describe physical, so that neither kind has any categorial priority in the job of depicting our mental life. So for "belief," "knowledge," "conception" and other cognitive terms: which uses of which primarily relate to occasions and which to tendencies is largely an empirical question.

I hope I have made it absolutely clear that I do not propose that we identify belief or any cognitive state of

2. "Ghosts and Categorial Mistakes," *Philosophical Studies,* VII (January-February, 1956), pp. 1-6.

mind with any bodily process. Readiness to act is not belief or any part of belief. Rather, it is the confused perception of being set to act, abstracted from its favorableness or unfavorableness to the object, which marks our belief. Since the whole state is intentional, there is no difficulty here in picking out what is believed as there certainly is in any behavioristic theory of cognition, and, since the type of reference is sentential or assertive, not nominative, we escape the anomaly of a supposedly physical and thus observable relation of belief to an object which may not exist.

Perhaps a word should also be devoted to the distinction between belief and what I have called assertion or claim. Every descriptive sentence embodies a claim: it is about its object in a way which can be either true or false. This is true of proxies for perceptions and even perceptions themselves. But we need not accept the claim, we may disbelieve it, even, again, in the case of perceptual experience. One can reject what one sees or hears—as being a dream, a distortion, an illusion. This would not be possible if belief and assertive reference were simply identical. The account of belief just given makes this distinction and also has a place for the personal involvement marking out belief. Belief includes assertive reference in the apprehension of the object; but besides this it involves a "dynamic background" formed of a confused perception of the body's readiness to act, whether favorably or unfavorably, to this object, or in disbelief the experience of an inhibition of such a readiness to act.

We can now, perhaps, make the dissimilarity between beliefs and feelings more specific. Beliefs are directed toward the existence of their objects; by abstraction from the favorableness or unfavorableness of our emotions they omit the evaluation of the objects always actually present in the emotions. They are directed to the facts, however we may feel about them. Our confused perception of our bodily readiness to act in any way toward the object "carries," in the non-conventional language of immediate experience, our assertion of the object's existence; our experience of inhibition of such tendencies to act "carries" our denial of the object's existence. Absence of any tendency to act is not disbelief but simply a nonexistence of belief. Beliefs can thus be two-valued (true or false) whereas feelings, as evaluative, are at least three-valued; disfavor is not the inhibition of favor but its opposite, and there are states in which there is an object but one's attitude toward it is neutral. It follows of course that beliefs are not concrete events but abstractions; indeed, so also are evaluations, as already intimated and to be pointed up presently.

11

Emotions As Evaluations

HUME WAS RIGHT, as against the Cambridge Plato-
nists. We have no purely intellectual apprehension of
a priori moral truths (or for that matter, of any other value
principles). Our value judgments finally reduce to emotions, to approvals and disapprovals which can be quite
appropriately described as feelings of pleasure and displeasure, namely those experienced upon a disinterested
viewing of their objects. But his argument was poor and
his analysis was wrong.

His main line of demonstration rested on the contention that our moral judgments affect our behavior whereas
our intellectual apprehensions do not; motivation to action
involves feelings, and knowledge is insufficient at least as
regards the ends of our conduct. This proof seems to me
weak. It easily becomes verbal: if we point out cases in
which new knowledge has modified a man's behavior, it is
tempting simply to assert, in reply, that the matter concerned the means of his action, not its ends, or that a
change of feelings must also have occurred. But if it really
is an empirical issue that could be settled by observations
or to which negative instances might be found, then it
clearly falls within the province of the psychology of motivation. It is notorious that Hume did not differentiate
psychological and epistemological problems, but we should
not follow his example in this regard. That moral judgments are essentially feelings of pleasure of a certain sort

is surely a categorial identification, not an empirical generalization. It needs some other form of argument than observations of motivation.

However, though Hume's reasoning is weak, we may perhaps grant it some weight (we shall return to this in connection with recent forms of the "emotive" theory). What is really bad is Hume's analysis. He tried to make out, in consonance with his general account of experience, that feelings have no reference to any objects, from which it follows, of course, that they make no claims. We noted earlier that he did not remain consistent in this position; indeed, on the very feelings now in discussion, namely, those of moral approval and disapproval, he used intentionalistic language. I personally think this was unavoidable, that one cannot take over from common speech such terms as "approval" and "disapproval" without, tacitly at least, giving them objects (one approves such-and-such conduct or expresses approval of so-and-so's behavior), so that, if made synonymous with "disinterested pleasure," correct usage requires a complement in this latter case, too (one is pleased with so-and-so's behavior, and so forth).

If Hume had followed this path so clearly marked by our everyday habits of speech his "emotivism" would not have had its skeptical consequences so shocking to the common mind. Our moral judgments unquestionably do say things and say them about their ostensible objects, and no view which reduces them to unmeaning events is acceptable to anyone with a commonsensical orientation. When one says that racial segregation is wrong, his judgment is about something and it is evaluative. The aphorism, "The unexamined life is not worth living," may be hyperbole, but it at least claims that it is good to examine one's life.

Moral, aesthetic and other evaluative judgments are probably as current in our daily intercourse as are descriptive and informational statements, nor do they seem to be in any greater danger of extinction as a result of axiological skepticism than are everyday characterizations of physical events as a consequence of epistemological subjectivism. It is wisdom on our part to try to understand them rather than to destroy them.

Conventional sentences of all kinds are capable of making evaluations, but value judgments are perhaps most clearly formulated in two varieties which I shall designate "value-predicative" and "normative." An example of the first is, "Self-examination is good," of the second, "Racial segregation ought to be terminated."

It was an earlier contention of mine (in *What Is Value?*), and is one to which I still hold, that the normative sentence reveals more explicitly and less misleadingly what is involved in our ordinary value-claims than does the value-predicative. This can be shown in several ways. If the valuing function is performed by a predicate-term, such as "good" in our instance, we discover in the grammar of its everyday use anomalies marking it off from descriptive predicates. In the case of descriptive predicates it is meaningful, however rare, to use exactly the same set except for one in characterizing two individuals. Suppose Muriel and Martha are identical twins; it would be sensible to describe them in precisely the same way save with the qualification, "But Muriel is a little stooped whereas Martha is not." But it would not be permitted to describe their moral character and conduct as exactly the same, making only the qualification, "But Muriel is good whereas Martha is not."

Again, value-predicates ride "piggy-back" on descriptive ones, and there seems to be no reciprocation of this

service. If I am told, "Muriel is good," I can properly
inquire, "In what respect, what about her is good?", indicating my supposition that her goodness is a matter of her
exemplification of other properties, such as honesty, in-
dustry and humility. But if I am informed that she is tall
I do not ask, "In what respect, what about her is tall?",
unless I have misunderstood my informer.

Furthermore, there seem to be two different ways in
which we can negate a value-predicate, whereas we would
normally accept only one for descriptions. If I say, "It is
not the case that self-examination is good," I may mean
either that it is bad or that it is neither good nor bad. If,
however, I claim, "It is not the case that self-examination
is difficult," I clearly am saying that it is easy. In common
speech the law of excluded middle does not appear to hold
for value-predications in the obvious way it does for factual
descriptions. Another way of putting this is to say that
value-predicates come paired—good-bad, right-wrong,
virtue-vice—whereas descriptive one-place- or quality-pred-
icates do not. This way of stating the matter is perhaps
a little too simple; there are complementary colors and opposite directions of pitch, as well as thermal contraries, but
these cannot be arranged through a neutral center in the
way characteristic of value-predicates.

Finally (though my list is not meant to be exhaustive),
value-predicates seem to embrace a reference to fact (particularly to the exemplification of the properties upon which
they ride "piggy-back") which is quite peculiar to them.
Self-examination is not judged good as a character; it is its
exemplification that is prized. It is not Muriel's honesty
but her being honest that is termed good. At first sight
common speech may not seem to bear me out on this. We
frequently hear clerics affirm that mercy is good, and old
ladies that lavender is beautiful, but if, in response to our

challenge that his theology has no place for mercy on God's part, the one were to reply, "Oh, I said that mercy is good; I did not mean that merciful acts are," or if, in answer to our query why she never selected anything lavender for herself or her house, the other were to explain, "I meant that lavender as a color is beautiful, not that anything colored lavender is," we would surely feel put upon. Such replies would show that these parties had seriously mistreated the idiom they had adopted.

The normative form, though not ideal in every way and frequently not appropriate to the demands of the concrete situation, is not systematically so misleading as the value-predicative. By having the evaluative factor appear as an auxiliary, our sentence is required to possess something else, something ordinarily descriptive, as a predicate. "Muriel should be humble (as indeed she is)" ascribes normatively to its subject an ordinary descriptive predicate ("humble"). This satisfies the need, appearing in the "piggy-back" character of value-predicates, of attaching value to the possession of some *other* property. And also to the *possession* of such a property, not to the property as an essence. When we say, "Muriel should be humble," we are not evaluating humility but Muriel's exemplification of it. Furthermore, this takes care of another, related anomaly when one uses the value-predicative form. We frequently wish to approve or disapprove something which isn't the case or we do not know is the case. We could of course use a complicated, subjunctive value-predicative form: "Muriel could be good—if she were to be humble," for example. This can be much more straightforwardly put in a normative, "Muriel ought to be humble." But the normative has a deeper advantage than its greater simplicity; it says something which the value-predicative sentence cannot. It asserts as present in the world, so to speak, a value which a sentence of the other kind can only affirm would be present in another state of affairs. The ought-to-be-so-and-so is claimed for this world, not for another where what ought to be, is.

This is connected, I admit, with a slight disadvantage. Ordinarily if I were to say, "Muriel ought to be humble," I would be taken to imply that she is not. If I wanted to affirm the opposite fact, I could supplement my normative, "Muriel ought to be humble and she is." But if I wanted to leave all description aside, I would have to say something like, "Whether she is or not, Muriel should be humble." It is unnecessary to point out that the value-predicative form cannot supply what we want, namely, a sentence type which allows us to say just the value-thing, without any tacit factual affirmation or denial. "It is fitting (to her sex) that Muriel be humble" might in certain circumstances do this, but it is a stilted form suitable only to moral pronouncements absent from ordinary moral conversation. But despite this involvement of the normative with a factual negative—perhaps in part because of it—this form shows how we do in daily life assert the value of some fact without asserting the fact, and grasping this is basic to an understanding of ordinary value judgments.

The double kind of negative in our value-thinking is not quite so readily displayed in the normative, though it might have been (the mechanism is there, so to say). Let me create a neologism. Suppose I wanted to deny "Muriel should be humble (whether she is or not)." This I could do in two mutually irreducible ways: by saying "Muriel ought not to be humble" (that is, she should display pride) or by stating "Muriel not-ought to be humble" (that is, she has no obligation in the matter). So far as I am aware, we do not in English have a value-term acting as an auxiliary verb to which a negative can be attached, as contrasted with

a negation of the descriptive verb or copula and predicative adjective with which it is used. Yet we frequently
wish to say the sort of thing this construction would, if we
had it, permit us to say. We can do this by using a noun,
which carries the value-element, qualified by a verbal
phrase introducing the descriptive factor. Thus against
"It is Muriel's duty to be humble" we can place either "It is
Muriel's duty not to be humble" or "It is not Muriel's duty
to be humble."

It would be of great aid in our analytical job if we had
a model language or two which would clarify the logic of
the value-segment of ordinary speech. Something is being
done along this line. It is too early to assess it and I am not
the one to do so. I am convinced, however, that some of
the characteristics to which I have alluded do mark out our
common value-talk, and their preservation should be a
desideratum for anyone undertaking the construction of
such an ideal language.

Up to this point in the present chapter, I have been
dealing with conventional evaluative speech. What corresponds to it in direct experience? Our whole approach
demands that we accept the proposition that something not
reducible to convention is expressed by our everyday evaluations; this, then, need not be here debated.

We might be tempted to jump immediately to the conclusion that there is some special kind of experience (to
carry on my metaphor, some distinct sort of "natural"
sentence or intention) not yet encountered in our analysis
which is thus expressed. There are those who have taken
this road (or so I interpret them). The moral sense school
did it in ethics; Clive Bell with his experience of significant
form followed a similar line in aesthetics.

I have little to say against this type of answer, mainly
perhaps because it is out of the current mode. But we

should note that it opens the door to all sorts of individual vagaries. If my moral sense disapproves certain practices as regards, say, gift-giving which yours approves, we seem to be at a dead-end, each resting on a conviction that the other's sense is perverted or perhaps not present and functioning at all, and of course we are in the same impasse if our feelings for significant form in the case, say, of a surrealist painting are in conflict. Then there are those (I happen to be one of them) who find no such unique forms of value-experience; it seems highhanded to throw out the evidence of these witnesses, particularly in cases in which they show high moral sensitivity or broad yet critical artistic appreciation. In short, this whole manner of approach promises little in the way of developing, in a socially acceptable fashion, our knowledge of value. Finally, there is Ockham's razor: if we can get along with fewer entities we should do so. I believe we can and advise that we examine what we have already found in experience.

I disclosed my preference some time ago. Of the two kinds of natural sentence or non-conventional intention we have discussed, perceptions lack important qualification for service as the originals of our conventional evaluative claims. We do not hear, see, taste, smell or otherwise sensibly perceive either moral or aesthetic values, whether as qualities or relations. If we did, then the anomalies of the value-predicative type of conventional sentence mentioned before would not obtain: value judgments would be and behave quite like predications of color or length. Not that perceptions are not present in value-experiences; rather, they aren't enough. I do not directly experience the evil of a man's conduct or the aesthetic poverty of an oil painting without perceiving (or imaging) the behavior or the picture. However, simply perceiving them, or more accurately stated, viewing any total experience of them abstractly as just a perception of them, is inadequate, omitting precisely the value-component we are seeking.

So I turn from perceptions to emotions, and here I meet with remarkable success. Emotions possess just the complexity of pattern we need. The normative value-sentence of everyday speech, particularly as supplemented by the neologism mentioned earlier, is very nicely matched by the structure of emotion as we have analyzed it. Corresponding to the "ought" or other valuational component acting as an auxiliary verb in the conventional normative, there is the confused perception of bodily changes in the emotion; correlated with the descriptive verbal phrase or the copula with predicate adjective in the former, there is the perception (anticipation or memory) of the exciting object in the latter. And in both cases the sentence is complex, not compound. "Muriel ought to be humble" does not say two things, "Muriel has a duty" and "Muriel is humble," but only one, that she has precisely the duty of being humble. The man's pleasure over his wife's return is not simply a set of two independent groups of perceptions, the bodily ones constituting his pleasure and those of the exciting object, namely, his wife's return; his emotion is a single experience with its own total intentionality—the somatic factor is directed towards the exciting object and gives it its emotional tone; he is pleased with his wife's return. Moreover, there is the three-valued character (to put it pseudo-logically) of sentences of each of these kinds. Just as Muriel may have the duty of being humble or of not being humble (that is, of being proud), or again may have no duty either way, so the man may be pleased with his wife's return, displeased with it (that is, he would be pleased with her non-return) or again feel no pleasure either way (that is, feel indifferent about her return).

So, then, I present my candidate. It is our emotions—and I refer to all of them, not some special class of moral and aesthetic ones—which are the elements in direct experience that make the basic value-claims.

On first thought it might seem plausible to restrict the experiential basis of our value-judgments to the calm emotions and the more settled attitudes. Such plausibility comes, I surmise, from a valid sense that, on the average, such feelings are more reliable than our stronger and more impetuous passions. I think they should be given more weight than the latter: we shall consider this when exploring coherence patterns of "justification," as I shall term it, of the value-claims embedded in our emotions. But that our more agitated and less judicious feelings have no validity or make no claims cannot be upheld on the intentional approach we have taken. They have the same design as our calmer states, and indeed often agree with them in their evaluations: violent hate of some injustice done may be replaced in time by a milder disapproval, but the two states agree in condemning the unjust act as evil.

It has long been recognized that emotions can be classified as for or against their objects, as friendly or hostile. Hate, anger, disgust, fear, regret, sorrow, displeasure are opposed to their objects. Love, delight, hope, pleasure, joy are in favor of theirs. True, within each class there are great differences. If we wish, we can go the whole distance and claim that every individual emotion is unique. This surely is true, but hardly of particular significance at this point. Every perception is likewise unique; in fact, whenever we assert or deny anything in conventional language, the actual occurrence of the symbols is something that happens only once. More specifically, then, an emotion taken as evaluative of its object does not assert of that object the possession of just the complex of somatic reverberations which marks out its special emotive character, as, for example, fear or disgust. Its evaluative dimension lies in its being favorable or unfavorable (or in some cases neutral) to its object.

That we have neutral feelings is important for us. Such feelings are unimportant in practical affairs since not associated with action, which probably accounts for the lack of a good name for them, "indifference," "unconcern," "apathy," "not-caring" being perhaps as acceptable as any. But it is a fact that we frequently do have a centralizing perception or a statement in conventional language conferring an object upon a total state in which the somatic background is neutral, being neither for nor against this object.

So emotions furnish what we seek. It is upon them, I contend, that our knowledge of value finally rests. Evaluative sentences in conventional language receive whatever probability they have from their truthfulness to emotions. They serve, so to speak, as the perceptions of this department.

I need not remark that the "truthfulness" to which I refer is not correctness of depiction but faithfulness of translation. Our moral and aesthetic judgments are not about our emotions; they are renditions of our emotions, having the same objects as our emotions have, saying (in part) exactly what our emotions say. They are expressions of emotion.

Putting it this way, however, points up a kind of anomaly. Have I not said that perhaps all and certainly many of the sentences we utter, taken in their concrete occurrence, express emotions? I have; and I accept the consequence that many sentences in ordinary speech that are not normative or value-predicative in form also express emotions. Does it not follow that many, if not all, of our everyday utterances are evaluative? I think it does, and I think that this is the proper way to view them. But does not this outcome destroy the whole distinction between declaration of fact and claim of value? Not at all.

When we assert some fact, we ordinarily do so for some purpose and with some emotional overtone. But our hearers, and we ourselves, can abstract from these and consider what is declared to be fact and whether it is fact. In doing so we neglect but do not deny the accompanying evaluation (which, of course, can be taken up at any time—"Why did you say that? Of course it's a fact, but why bring it up?," etc.) Our specifically evaluative language is distinguished by the characteristic of not being declarative of fact, or if it is, of subordinating this to the role of specifying what is being evaluated. I am quite ready to admit that, taken in their concrete occurrence, a declarative and a normative may do almost exactly the same things: "Muriel is not humble" may express and convey the evaluation that she ought to be, and "Muriel should be humble" may be understood to imply the declaration that she is not. However, these same words may be used on other occasions with other unverbalized connotations so that it is quite legitimate to take them abstractly in what they commonly or most frequently say. And so taken, there are sentences which are not, primarily, declarative of fact but evaluative of it (or of possible fact).

So, now, we come to the question, why should this be? Why, besides the evaluation concretely involved in all or almost all our conventional everyday language, do we have special verbal forms to express it? Strictly, it is not my job as a philosopher to answer this: it would accord with professional proprieties simply to point out that we do. But I shall not be that pedantic, for I, too, love to psychoanalyze my fellows.

First, I think that Charles Stevenson, though seriously deficient in his analysis of "emotive meaning," is quite insightful as regards the motivation of much of our evaluative language. Expressing our emotions by tone of voice and other non-verbal means may not be as effective in persuading others to feel and act as we do as couching our evaluations in predicates or sentential forms reserved for this purpose. Moreover, there is the personal factor. In taking experiences as perceptions of external events we abstract from their somatic components; this, of course, we cannot do when viewing them as emotions. The favoring, disfavoring or not caring about something are ours, borne by the confused sense we have of processes in our own, individual bodies. In wishing to escape from this and from the pathetic fallacy to which it easily leads, we invent terms and sentence-forms that will drop out, as much as possible, the involvement of our evaluations with our personal selves in order to obtain social "objectivity." Finally (and this constitutes my major emphasis in this speculative psychology of speech), we often want to make, discuss and criticize precisely the value-claim found in our emotions. Why not formulate this abstractly, in its own right? This really seems to me a rather common motivation despite the omission or even disparagement of reference to it by many contemporary linguistic analysts.

One last sociological question: Why have most objectivists and non-naturalists in value theory been so anxious to hide the emotional character of our evaluations? The more conservative of them perhaps could not break away from the ascetic element in our Christian tradition: the passions can only be evil and misleading; they cannot point out the true values. Another reason, no doubt at heart inconsistent with that just suggested, lies in the conviction, shared by almost all subjectivists and naturalists, that emotions make no claims, have no intentions, are to be treated simply as events. In the third place, there may be a few who have been primarily dissuaded by the belief that, though emotions do evaluate, there is no way to substantiate their evaluations; hence they are epistemically worthless.

This last group deserves a hearing. The mere fact that our immediate experience makes value-claims is not by itself sufficient to justify those claims. Moreover, such claims are frequently in conflict, some emotions favoring exactly what others disfavor. Some method of determining relative probabilities must be found if we are to accept emotions as furnishing the basis of our knowledge of value. This leaves us with a project still to be carried out.

12

The Legitimacy of Emotions

FREQUENTLY we ask whether under the circumstances in which it occurred a certain emotion is legitimate or justified. What we mean is, is its occurrence proper, that is, ought it to have occurred. This is basically a normative or value-question in its own right (no different from a similar question about an action). But we may also be interested in the validity or correctness of an emotion. This is a question about its evaluation of its object. It is not a normative but a semantical matter. Is the object hateful or lovable as the emotion takes it to be; is it worthy of being an object of the emotion in question? Here the value with which one is concerned is not that of the emotion itself (that is, that it has occurred) but of the object towards which one feels the emotion.

The first question, on the view I have sketched, is about the appropriateness of the emotion to the circumstances in which it occurs. This is, on this view, to be determined by emotions directed to it (that is, to its occurrence in just its circumstances). It may be wrong to feel a certain emotion even when this emotion is legitimate (when it evaluates its object correctly). An analogy in the case of factual evidence may help make this clear. Suppose I spy on someone's private life. I may then have veridical perceptions which I never should have had, which are themselves unjustified. Not every mode of verifying factual beliefs is legitimate. So for ways of "verifying" value-judgments.

In the last analysis we do this through feelings (just as we verify descriptive assertions through perceptions), but not every occurrence of an emotion, even when the emotion is corroborated by others so that it may be taken to present the proper evaluation of the object, is itself proper. Comparable to the evil of spying on another (despite the veridicalness of one's perceptions) is that of falling in love with the other's wife (despite the eminent worthiness of the woman to be loved). Now it might be said that what is wicked in each case is not the experience itself (the seeing or the loving) but its consequences. This may be true, for it is the occurrence in the circumstances of the perceptual, or again of the emotional, experience that is bad. Abstractions, and perceptions and feelings as intentions are abstractions, are never good or evil. But are not hallucinatory perceptions and wrong emotions inherently bad? No. Circumstances can be conceived in which either might be good, or at least better on the whole than its opposite. Not every increase in truth (whether as to fact or value) is itself a good.

We shall be no more concerned with evaluating emotions than with evaluating behavior, works of art or anything else. Our interest in emotions is not as objects but as forms of evaluation. By their "legitimacy" will be meant the soundness or correctness of their evaluation; by their "justification," the evidence for their legitimacy or the way in which one can make out that they are legitimate or the criterion of legitimacy.

Compared with its companion, "What is the truth of a descriptive statement?", the problem, "What is the legitimacy of an evaluative claim?," has provoked amazingly little thought. Unquestionably a major cause of this phenomenon is that our question has not been generally distinguished in any clear fashion from its companion. The questions are analogous and should be so viewed, but they are not identical as I have already indicated and hope to bring out more explicitly later. That they have been badly confused is quite evident in many discussions of truth, especially in those oriented toward a coherence- or verification-type theory.

Generally those philosophers who have said that truth is coherence have claimed that goodness and beauty are, also. When they talk this way I think they are involved in several muddles at once, but a confusion of legitimacy with truth appears to be included. In any case, their way of speaking brings before us the possibility of a coherence theory of legitimacy. May we not suppose that legitimacy is some kind of coherence?

This question immediately calls to mind objections we found against an affirmative answer to the analogous query about truth. First there is its ambiguity. What is to cohere and what is to be its coherence on this suggestion? If the answer to the former is "the world" and to the latter "a kind of harmony or absence of any real discord," I would point out that the discussion has forsaken epistemology for ontology. Suppose the supreme value to be a world-harmony; the consequence would be that a judgment making this claim would be legitimate, but not that its legitimacy would be the harmony. Indeed, quite the opposite, for the harmony would lie in the value, the legitimacy in the claim. In order that the claim be significant, it must at least be possible to entertain the counter-claim, that a world in which there was some discord might be better than a world with none. This being so, some method of justifying these opposite claims, that is, of making out their relative probability, is required, and so we see that the whole epistemic question is begged, for justification in this sense is directed to the legitimacy of the claims, not to anything else about them. Incidentally, I think that few of us, even in this strife-torn world, want to affirm that degree of value is exactly proportionate to degree of harmony, and fewer still that to deny it is self-contradictory.

Avoiding this intrusion into the domains of ontology, we might specify that the coherence which is to define legitimacy obtain between value-claims. What then is it? It certainly must be narrower than freedom from contradiction in a logical sense. No one would admit that every value-claim that is uninvolved in self-contradiction is legitimate. We might try to get the largest system of such claims that is free from internal contradiction and say that its constituents are legitimate. But would we be willing to identify their legitimacy with their membership in this set? I think any commonsensical consideration of actual cases would soon dissuade us from such an admission. Surely when I aver the legitimacy of the claim, "Segregation is wrong," I am not simply saying that it is a member of a set, however large, of mutually consistent claims. What more, then, should be added to transform consistency into the desired coherence? There seems to be no candidate ready at hand, but even if there were, it would not perform the trick of changing the resultant coherence into legitimacy. On the one hand, we could always significantly ask, "Are the constituents of such-and-such a group of value-claims, however coherent, legitimate?" On the other, coherence is not redundant in a way in which legitimacy is. "The claim, 'Segregation is wrong,' is a legitimate one" is equivalent to "Segregation is wrong," but " 'Segregation is wrong' is coherent with certain other value-claims" is not, no matter what these other claims may be. Lastly, coherence is usually considered to be a matter of degree, legitimacy is not. The disapprobation, "Segregation is wrong," either is legitimate or it is not. This of course must be kept distinct from the question whether there are degrees of value, from, for example, the question of how wrong segregation may be as compared with other evils.

Some pragmatists (I have William James in mind) in identifying truth with verification or the possibility of carrying it out, have obviously thought of it in value-terms, as something satisfying and therefore good. James explicitly says that the true is anything good in the way of belief. Here, as with the coherence philosophers, I think we have a reprehensible mixing of epistemology and ontology (not to mention morality), but we are thereby led to a second possibility for our consideration. May we not define the legitimacy of a value-claim as its verification or verifiability (or to avoid confusion with truth, as its "justification" or "justifiability," as I shall say)?

I think not. This way seems to be blocked by obstacles similar to those just noted in our discussion of a coherence definition of legitimacy. In whatever manner we set up justification, it would seem desirable to have it, like its associate, verification, capable of degree; in any case, as an empiricist I find myself committed to this and shall not argue it at this point. But, if we have been right, legitimacy is all or none. Moreover, the affirmation of legitimacy is reiterative in a way in which an assertion of justification is not. To say, "I am engaged in justifying the claim that segregation is wrong" (or that I have been, will be or could be, or that anyone else is or might be) is to assert something quite different from, "Segregation is wrong," but "Segregation is wrong" and "The claim that segregation is wrong is legitimate" amount to the same thing.

Besides these obstructions to the identification of legitimacy with justification, there is another not particularly analogous to any stopping us from identifying it with coherence. James saw that on his view truth is man-made.

Something similar may be said of our present theory of legitimacy. We institute and carry out justifications of various value-claims. It follows that if the legitimacy of those claims is their justification, it is something we produce. This is almost as shocking a consequence to common sense as the analogous one for truth. We can hardly tolerate, "I have just made [or am just about to make] 'Segregation is wrong' legitimate."

Finally, although perhaps all my other objections are just variations on this theme, we in ordinary discourse distinguish between what I have called the legitimacy and the justification of an assertion of value. This appeals to me as a strong argument, though I admit that it is somewhat weakened by the absence of a uniform, current terminology (which I have filled in with the words "legitimacy" and "justification") comparable to "truth" and "verfication" as applied to declarations of fact. Perhaps, then, I should put my point as follows: everyday thought is carried on in a framework involving two quite different concepts relative to value-claims, one comparable to their truth or correctness, the other to their verification or establishment. Suppose I say, "Under the circumstances, Jane should have broken her promise." It would be entirely proper for you to reply, "You may be right, but how can you show it?" If I am right, my judgment is legitimate; if I haven't shown that I am right, it is unjustified (in the present use of these terms).

Carrying further our method of analogy, can we not hope for a theory of legitimacy analogous to our correspondence theory of truth? I believe we can, but we must face dangers like those we encountered in the latter, plus an additional one arising from this very comparison.

It is unobjectionable to say that legitimate value-claims correspond to the values they affirm. It is quite wrong, however, to try to define "legitimacy" in terms of this correspondence, for the relation holds between the classes, whereas it is the individual claims that are legitimate. What we should say, then, is that it is the relation of legitimacy obtaining between the individual claims and the values they assert which generates the correspondence between the classes, keeping in mind that it is not altogether proper to call this a "relation" (we do not ordinarily speak of a value-claim as "legitimate of" something but merely as "legitimate").

Despite the striking analogy between legitimacy and truth it is of first importance that they not be confused. We are helped here by noting that the correlations they generate are different. Thinking back to what we have already seen, declarative sentences have only a single form of negation, normative have two. I negate "Muriel is humble" by saying "Muriel is not humble," but I can deny "Muriel has the duty to be humble" either by claiming "Muriel has the duty not to be humble" or by alleging "Muriel has no duty in the matter of humility." Now we ordinarily suppose that the semantics of truth and falsity must go along with the grammar of affirmation and negation so that "Muriel is humble" is true if, and only if, Muriel is humble, and it is false if, and only if, she is not. We would want, I am sure, something similar for the semantics of legitimacy, that is, we would want three alternatives so that we could take care of the double way of negation. I suggest, although I am not too happy about the terms, that we say "Muriel has the duty to be humble" is "legitimate" if, but only if, she has this duty, that it is "illegitimate" if, and only if, she has the duty not to be humble and finally that the claim is "non-legitimate" when, yet only when, she has no duty about humility.

On this way of viewing it, the correspondence between value-claims and values is more complex than that between declarations of facts and facts.   Here is a rather crude analogy: we enter the room when the light is on but do not when it is not; we go when the traffic light is green, stop when it is red, proceed with caution if it shows yellow. The analogy is crude because we have no way of cross-combining the motions and the lights, whereas we need ways of uniting grammar and semantics so that we can speak of negations as well as affirmations as true or false, and have the same freedom, *mutatis mutandis,* in speaking of value-claims.

For truth we have a settled tradition to guide us, and one quite agreeable with common speech.   As between a declaration of fact and its denial, one must be true and the other false, so that we can say that the truth of either is equivalent to the negation of the other and the falsity of either to the affirmation of the other.   This is suggested, though not formulated, by the truth-table:

"Muriel is humble"	"Muriel is not humble"
is true	is false
is false	is true

For legitimacy we do not have a tradition in logic we can follow, nor is common speech articulate or even consistent.   I put down a "legitimacy-table" in the hope not that it will set up a tradition in logic or crystallize the thought-patterns of everyday life but that it will help make clear the sort of correspondence I have in mind as perhaps vaguely present in common thinking as it relates to values and value-claims.

"Muriel has the duty to be humble"	"Muriel has the duty not to be humble"	"Muriel has no duty about being humble"
is legitimate is illegitimate is non-legitimate	is illegitimate is legitimate is non-legitimate	is non-legitimate is non-legitimate is legitimate

I hope that this table will be viewed with a tolerant eye. So far as our value-thinking in ordinary situations has fairly definite features, I think the schematism is true to them. This applies, I feel, to the left and the middle columns and to the bottom line. Where the table may strike one as rather contrived, namely, in the upper and middle entries in the right-hand column, it seems to reflect a lack of explicitness in our everyday habits. Yet even here I can make something of a case for it. The only other plausible alternative would be to have both entries at these places "is illegitimate," but it is quite undesirable to have two of our three mutually exclusive alternatives illegitimate under the same value-conditions. Similar reasoning does not apply to the double occurrence of "is non-legitimate" in the bottom line in view of the primary meaning of this phrase, which is precisely reflected in this bottom line itself. That there are two quite different conditions under which "Muriel has no duty about being humble" is non-legitimate appears entirely acceptable, for in each she would have a duty, namely, when "Muriel has the duty to be humble" is legitimate and when "Muriel has the duty not to be humble" is.

It may be noted that the table embodies for legitimacy something comparable to the laws of contradiction and excluded middle for truth: under any given value-conditions only one of our alternative value-claims is legitimate but, on the other hand, at least one is.

As I have said, I make no large claims for this legitimacy-table. Nevertheless, if it does in some fashion agree with our everyday patterns of value-assertion, then it can help us realize that legitimacy, though in many ways analogous to truth, is in others quite dissimilar and so should not be identified with the latter. But now I must point out that this whole approach runs into a serious danger. When we speak of truth and legitimacy, together with their respective alternatives, as correspondences with facts and values, and their appropriate negates, we appear headed toward a most questionable ontological commitment. We seem to be entangled in the assumption that, corresponding to true and false descriptive sentences, there are facts and non-facts, and correlated with legitimate, illegitimate and non-legitimate value judgments, there are positive values, negative ones and value-indifferences. What bothers me right now is not so much the factor of negativity, which must, I am convinced, be given some ontological status in both realms, but the almost irresistible temptation associated with the language of correspondence to think of facts and values as particulars. Most of the correspondences we assert are between classes of observable individual entities —husbands and wives, people and their name-cards, and so on. Now, if I am right, in neither truth nor legitimacy is this the case. In the aspects relevant to the correspondences we are discussing, neither factual declarations nor value-claims are subject to sensory observation. Facts and values are in a comparable state. They cannot be put alongside our sentences affirming them, for we can get at them, in the last analysis, only as the objects of those sentences.

It helps if we return to an insight we had before Neither truth nor legitimacy can be defined as a correspondence; only classes can correspond to one another, whereas it is single sentences that are true or legitimate. The only proper form of a correspondence theory in either case is one which specifies that truth or legitimacy, as the case may be, is a relation that generates the appropriate correspondence.

In discussing truth we concluded that we could not define it but that we could characterize it as a "relation" which generates a certain correspondence which we called the "truth-correspondence," correlating certain sentences with the facts they declare. I think our analysis leads towards a similar outcome in the case of legitimacy; certainly I find myself unable at present to define it, but I am willing to characterize it as a "relation" which generates a certain correspondence (suggested by the legitimacy-table I constructed and to be called the "legitimacy-correspondence"), correlating certain sentences with the values they claim. If one could formulate a satisfactory definition of either, I think it would have to include some reference to the declaration of fact or to the description of individuals through properties predicated of them, in the one case, and to the claiming of value or the appropriateness of an exemplification of certain properties by individuals, in the other. Moreover, I think the semantic claim in the generating relation in either instance is far more basic than the correspondence set up, although the latter, by its characteristic form, does reflect light back on what generated it.

With these dangers and qualifications in mind, we may describe the position here advocated as a "correspondence theory of legitimacy." Does it not, if thought through, lead into skepticism? I believe no more so than in the comparable instance of our correspondence theory of truth. I think there is no need here of a review of confusions similar to those pointed out in connection with that theory. However, the correspondence theory of legitimacy does issue in probabilism. We have no certainty concerning the legitimacy of any value-claim. But this admission is not as damaging as it may sound at first if we can find, as I think we can, reasonable methods capable of establishing different probabilities of legitimacy for conflicting value-claims.

13

The Justification of Emotions

NO DOUBT we face in the present chapter the job which is psychologically the most crucial for the type of epistemology of value we have been developing. If all our knowledge of value is to rest upon the claims embodied in actually occurring emotions, it is of first importance that some of these claims be in some degree justified and, in cases of conflict between them, that some be justified to a greater degree than others. I fear that the performance will not appear as exciting as the statement of the task, for it will amount essentially to a pointing up of procedures familiar to us in everyday life but until now quite generally considered unworthy of the philosopher's attention. Yet the choice is inevitable, being dictated by our common-sensical approach. However, we need not apologize for it; it makes possible a happy combination not too frequently found in value theory, namely, of objectivism with empiricism.

Let us explore the analogy of the justification of our value-claims to the verification of our factual assertions. In each case they are directed towards a semantical property of the sentences involved, one being a matter of the probability of a statement's truth, the other, of a judgment's legitimacy. Following common sense, we found ourselves committed, granting appropriate qualifications, to a correspondence theory of each of these latter, that is, of truth and legitimacy. Trusting the same leadership, we developed certain coherence patterns for perceptual verification; I think we can do something similar in the case of justification. However, just as legitimacy is more complex than truth, so we may expect justification to be more involved than verification.

For the most part, this greater complexity will be noted in connection with specific patterns of coherence, but there are two aspects of it which demand attention at the start. First there is a rather obvious matter. Our feelings evaluate facts, actual or possible. Consequently, before we can consider the justificatory weight of these evaluations we must be clear about the facts evaluated, about the objects of the feelings. Although for the purpose of understanding the character of evaluation we treated it as suspending factual assertion, this is frequently not the case in actual experience. Thus our emotions may be literally mistaken about their objects. Othello was thus wrong in his feelings concerning the love of Desdemona for Cassio. We, with our separation of the evaluative and descriptive claims, can clarify the situation by admitting that Othello's evaluation may have been quite sound but he was mistaken about the occurrence of the fact so evaluated. Of course the truth is not in actual life always so obvious as in a play. Still, though we cannot be sure who is right, we can distinguish disagreement about the facts from difference in evaluation of them, and to deal intelligently with the latter means we have resolved the former, at least tentatively and for the sake of the valuative argument.

Second, there is a more subtle matter. Perceptions are more abstract than emotions; if I am right, they are emotions taken in a certain way, that is, omissive of their somatic components. True, emotions when considered as evaluations are also treated abstractly, but in this case the confused experience of bodily changes is not completely disregarded; its favorableness, unfavorableness or indifference towards the object of the whole state is retained, for it is just this which constitutes the evaluative factor. This greater concreteness of bodily experience weakens its epistemic worth. I am not thinking merely nor mainly of the additional possibility of error to be found in our bodily experience itself. This is, of course, present; we may misperceive bodily occurrences even in waking life and, indeed, so badly that, for example, an unfavorable response may be misread for an indifferent or favorable one, as a study of abnormal psychological phenomena will show. But this is a relatively minor matter for our purposes and must be passed by.

What I have in mind is that the somatic factor in emotion is always an experience of the body of the person emotionally moved. If he takes care, he can avoid the pathetic fallacy of ascribing the complex of his visceral, muscular and other inner changes as he experiences them to the outer, exciting object, but still the approval, disapproval or evaluative neutrality are borne by these modifications. The difference from perception is not of course absolute; one only sees things from one's location, hears them with one's orientation, and so on; moreover, what one perceives is often to an unascertainable degree determined by one's feelings—anxiety, hope, nausea can make a great difference. Yet the central fact that one evaluates through or by means of one's bodily feelings brings in a greater factor of personal error than exists in the case of more abstract perception. This is reflected in the larger quantity of disagreement about felt values than perceived facts. However, it does not follow that our situation is hopeless. Although with intellectuals it is something of a commonplace to suppose there can be no dispute concerning taste, this is not so in popular thought (nor even, I suspect, for these same intellectuals when discussing concrete issues in morals, politics or art). It is well enough in trivial matters and for politeness' sake to say, "Oh, it's all a matter of taste"; not so, however, when the issue is genocide as practiced by the Nazis or the relative merits of T. S. Eliot and Edgar Guest as poets.

Common sense, then, is on my side: we can and must trust our feelings for values, but not equally. When they disagree some are more reliable than others. But to make this out more specifically, we must note in cursory fashion some of the coherence patterns we all quite regularly, though usually unconsciously, respect when putting value judgments to the test. I admit that by pointing some of these up and giving them abstract formulation I am "clarifying" our everyday habits of mind. I shall not pause to justify this, however, since I undertook a similar job in connection with perception.

Let us begin by granting to each actually occurring emotion a small but positive inherent probability of being legitimate. This is increased or decreased as we find that it does or does not fit into certain patterns of coherence with other feelings about the same object. And here we must quickly add "in some respect," for we may have several feelings about the same object at once. Not long ago I saw the annual exhibit of current Japanese art, Nittenbijutsu. Generally, I had a curious feeling of disapproval of the imitativeness of Western art in form and subject-matter combined with approval of the daring experimentation with color. This qualification is especially important in the case of my supposed disagreements of feelings; the emotions may be quite irrelevant since, though directed to the same over-all object, they may evaluate it in different respects.

On the other hand, we must not suppose two emotions to be irrelevant on the grounds that one of them is a state of indifference towards an object favored or disfavored by the other. We have already sufficiently noted that a state of emotional indifference towards an object must be distinguished from a sheer absence of feeling, that is, from an experience in which the thing in question does not serve as an object at all; it is usually a mild emotion, but it may on occasion, particularly on moral issues, be relatively strong. Thus it hardly needs remarking that a given feeling (say one of approval) may be opposed by a feeling of either of two contrary kinds towards the same object in some one respect (say one of disapproval or of indifference). The probability that your feeling that Muriel should be humble is legitimate would be lowered by my sense of neutrality as well as by a third party's feeling that she should not be.

A further complication arises from the inclusion of a factual reference (whose assertiveness may be considered suspended) in all evaluation. We favor or disfavor that something be the case, that some individual exemplify some property or enter some relation with other individuals. We earlier encountered a number of problems in connection with what I called "the empirical negative." Some properties, such as colors, tend to fall into sets that are incompatible with one another so far as exemplification by the same individual is concerned. We saw that this incompatibility cannot define the empirical negative, for it presupposes it: my pencil's being yellow does not constitute its not being blue—the world might have been made so that my pencil could have been both yellow and blue at once, and indeed it is so made that the pickle I ate for lunch was both sour and salty. To put it paradoxically, the empirical negative requires a positive absence of a property and is not reducible to the presence of an incompatible one. Nevertheless, we frequently do assume the incompatibility of properties, so that, for example, I am satisfied that my pencil is not blue by perceiving it to be yellow.

Now this factual incompatibility does in a way enter our evaluations, although its negative impact here is even softer than in our descriptive assertions. Obviously my approval of the saltiness of the pickle does not conflict with my favoring its being sour, for the pickle can be both. But my new coat cannot be both brown and blue. Am I in contradiction with myself if I approve both colors (I mean, of course, to distinguish this from an I-don't-care attitude)? I would, naturally, be at odds with myself if I both approved and disapproved its being brown. But need I disapprove its being brown simply because I approve its being blue? I think not. Common sense allows a tolerant form of evaluation as well as an intolerant. If the question is about what is best or what ought to be, then factual incompatibility of alternatives sets up a value-incompatibility to go with it. If I favor a brown coat as best, then I do get into disagreement with myself if I also like a blue one as most attractive. And since in action we often must choose between incompatible alternatives, there is understandable pressure upon everyday thought on moral matters to make intolerant evaluations, as evidenced by the prevalence of such concepts as one's duty, the right course of action and so on. Nevertheless, more tolerant forms are allowed, especially in the area of aesthetic appropriateness.

I suggest that we conclude that approvals directed towards factually incompatible alternatives may, but need not, be in disagreement, and that where they are, we mark their type of disagreement by calling it "indirect," in contrast with the "direct" disagreement between any pair in the set: approval, disapproval, indifference towards one and the same factual possibility.

Along with indirect disagreement we must allow, when the evaluation is intolerant, the possibility of indirect agreement. To be clear about this, think again of the empirical negative. Suppose my pencil must have some color but can have only one (a rather common assumption). Then to say that it is not blue implies that it is yellow or red or some other color. Applying this to evaluations of the most appropriate color for my new coat, we should say that disapproval of its being brown is in agreement with approval of its being some other color.

The combinations that seem to fit best our everyday intolerant way of thinking are typified, it seems to me, in the tables I have constructed, the first showing combinations of attitudes (represented on the same line in the two columns) which are in conflict and lower one another's probability, the second giving pairs that are mutually corroborative.

TABLE OF INDIRECT DISAGREEMENT OF ATTITUDES

It is best that my new coat be brown	It is best that my new coat be blue or green or some other color (than brown)
approval	approval
approval	indifference
disapproval	disapproval
disapproval	indifference
indifference	approval
indifference	disapproval

TABLE OF INDIRECT AGREEMENT OF ATTITUDES

It is best that my new coat be brown	It is best that my new coat be blue or green or some other color (than brown)
approval disapproval indifference	disapproval approval indifference

We are now ready to observe in a cursory fashion and by way of illustration what may happen to the inherent probability of an evaluation as embodied in some emotion when that emotion is brought into relation with others evaluative of the same object in some common respect. In general, of course, its probability is increased if these other evaluations agree with it, decreased if they disagree. However, we can be rather more specific if we look at the actual coherence patterns controlling our everyday thinking. These are even more interlaced than the principles determining the reliability of perception, so I think I am justified in abstracting and idealizing them.

First, there is the principle of quantitative corroboration: the larger the number of feelings evaluatively agreeing with a given one, the greater the probable legitimacy of that one. Professor Shizuichi Shimimisse, Dr. Richard Edwards and I recently visited the home of Mr. Inshyo Domoto. One of the paintings of that artist, uniting elements of Japanese calligraphy with western abstract tendencies, struck a particularly responsive chord in me. I felt fortified in my approval when both my friends expressed agreement with me.

Second, there is corroboration through variety in non-evaluative constituents of emotions: agreeing emotions add more to one another's probability if their perceptual constitutents other than in the respect evaluated show greater variety.   At the Nittenbijutsu exhibit I liked very much a lacquered screen with a bold design of yellow sunflowers against a black background.   My feeling was corroborated when I returned the same day and found I still admired it, but not so much so as it was when I revisited the museum on another day, when there were more spectators, my general bodily tonus was appreciably different, I viewed it sitting rather than standing and still found, despite these divergences in accompanying factors, that I esteemed it. This criterion is perhaps difficult to distinguish in practice from others, especially from the next to be mentioned, but I believe it is different.   In particular, I think we should place under it the greater significance we commonly assign to emotional agreement between different people as contrasted with the agreement in emotional responses of the same person on different occasions, when no question of relative discriminative powers or emotional sensitivity is involved.   The matter resolves itself, or so it appears to me, into the greater likelihood of there being a larger variety of perceptual constituents, especially somatic ones, when the emotions are those of different persons.   Something of this is no doubt to be found in Adam Smith's impartial spectator (although other criteria are probably at work here as well). When we assume the "role of the other," as George Mead phrased it, our total perspective shifts, so that if we come out with an agreeing evaluation we can rightly put more confidence in it than if we simply continued with the same feeling in our own person.

Third, there is the principle of maximum perceptual discrimination in the respect evaluated.   This pattern can perhaps be most simply stated in terms of conflicting feelings. Of two disagreeing evaluations, that one is most probably legitimate which embraces the greatest perceptual discrimination of properties in the respect evaluated. This can be generalized for conditions and persons: of two such feelings, that one is most probably legitimate which occurs under circumstances regularly allowing more discrimination in the respect involved, and something similar is true, with appropriate changes, of the relative powers of discrimination of the individuals whose feelings conflict. Suppose two people disagree about a Bach fugue, one enraptured by its rich pattern of sound, the other repelled by it as a cold intellectual exercise. If we find that the first has followed the theme as taken up by different voices, traced its variations through inversions, augmentations and so on, whereas the second cannot even recognize it when repeated, we quite naturally put more faith in the feelings of the first than in those of the second. This principle offers justification of the educational practice of giving knowledge of an art form in order to increase critical appreciation of art works in that form. There is a point beyond which greater perceptual discrimination frequently conflicts with emotional sensitivity, but that is not at the early stage when popular "hits" are disapproved because of their complete lack of subtlety but at the later one when evaluation is wholly determined by technical virtuosity or novelty. And lest I give the impression that this criterion applies to aesthetic values only, I suggest we think about the varying abilities of individuals to perceive the impact of their actions upon the lives and feelings of others. I am acquainted with a philosopher who is quite unable to discriminate between the reactions of his avid admirers and the good form observed by others. I think I am in line with common sense in questioning the reliability of his invariable self-approval.

Fourth, there is the criterion of emotional sensitivity. In practice it is difficult to distinguish this from our third pattern, but they need not be confused theoretically, the one being a matter of discrimination of features of the object of the emotion, the other, of differential somatic response to these. It goes without saying that a sensitive person must be a discriminative one, but the converse, though true in many instances, need not be and is not always the case. An individual with great powers of discrimination in some respect, say that of color and color-combination, may for some odd reason not have the emotional sensitivity usually associated with it; he may for example feel quite indifferent about the colors displayed by anything he experiences. Roughly stated, of two disagreeing evaluations, that one is more trustworthy which is experienced by the person who ordinarily is more sensitive emotionally or which occurs under conditions which are commonly associated with greater sensitivity. As already noted, "greater emotional sensitivity" refers to greater differentiation in the evaluation of discriminated properties of some one respect. This is not equivalent to a larger variety of emotions; it is a matter of the abstract character of emotions as evaluative (their favorableness, unfavorableness or neutrality). Nor should it be confused with intensity of emotion or with a low threshold of emotional stimulation. Highly emotional people, those with emotionally explosive personalities, ordinarily have a very low degree of emotional sensitivity. Bishop Butler's advice that we put our faith in the approvals and disapprovals we experience during a "cool hour" was and is sound and eminently commonsensical; such a condition promotes both perceptual discrimination and emotional sensitivity. Neurotic states are highly unreliable not because abnormal (the appreciation of a profound and sensitive critic may be even more abnormal in the sense of rare), but because emotionally undifferentiated (the depressed person disfavors everything he experiences, the manic approves all that happens).

Fifth, there is the relevance of the emotion to the respect being evaluated. It may be entirely irrelevant, as already mentioned, in which case it has no justificatory weight. But it may have a partial relevance less than that, for example, of some other emotion. This is possible because the respects in which we evaluate objects are more or less complex and overlapping. Suppose we have several disfavorable feelings about a painting, say the 1946 Francis Bacon aptly described in *Masters of Modern Art* in the words: "Surrounded by butchered sides of beef, this human carnivore stands on a chromium-plated rostrum with multiple microphones. The lower part of his head with its vermilion stubble glistens in the spotlight but an umbrella shades the upper part—if any." One is simply plain horror. Another is distaste for such subject-matter for a work of art. A third is a sense of dislike of the clashing reds, violets, purples used. A fourth is a general uneasiness, a feeling that the painting "doesn't come off"—that it too directly represents a disturbing hallucination to be susceptible of that psychical distancing necessary to aesthetic appreciation. If the evaluation we seek is that of the painting as a work of art, the fourth is the most relevant and thus the most justificatory of a negative evaluation. The first is wholly irrelevant, since it is a feeling for the subject represented, not the painting. The second and third are somewhat relevant, since choice of subject-matter and use of color are parts or phases of the total work of art.

This fifth pattern of coherence helps relieve the abstractness of our account of the experiential basis of our knowledge of value. Although here, too, it is only in the one dimension of favor-indifference-disfavor that emotions are considered, still their variety can be indirectly brought in through the variety and complexity of the respects in which they evaluate their objects. Objects of aesthetic appreciation and of moral judgment are very complicated entities, and our feelings about them differ in being directed to partially different aspects of them; thus the qualitative wealth of our feelings about ostensibly the same thing has some epistemic significance.

Last in my list, which does not pretend to be exhaustive, is the postulate of regularity. I think the common mind assumes that nature is uniform in the region of values as well as in that of fact. This is undoubtedly true of our thinking about morals. It is revealed in the impartial spectator of Adam Smith and even more strikingly in Kant's categorical imperative. We are not to make exceptions for ourselves or for our friends; a moral rule is binding upon everyone alike. It might seem more questionable when the subject is art. I personally would not like to find myself favoring academicism and opposed to experimentation, and I surely deplore an overhasty tendency to set up critical canons. Perhaps we should grant some difference in the authority of our postulate in different areas of value. Still, I think it does apply to some extent everywhere, with the consequence that we can take those evaluations to be more reliable which fit with more value-laws as determined by other appraisals of similar objects in the respect or respects involved.

Perhaps a word is demanded on the subject of conflicts between these patterns in specific applications. Such conflicts do occur. I offer no general principle for ranking them in such cases. As with the parallel clashes of criteria of perceptual reliability, we must finally either suspend judgment or determine the matter by decision. The latter procedure need not be completely arbitrary; we can follow the lead of those with greater experience and skill as attested by how well they have settled previous, similar issues. This sounds weak and vague, and it is, but it is the predicament we are actually in.

14

Generalizations of Emotive Evaluations

THE POSTULATE of value-regularity is deeply embedded in the categories of everyday thought. That it is, is witnessed by the acceptance in every culture of moral rules and artistic canons. The fact that there is intercultural disagreement on them should give us pause; generally, it has resulted not so much in a doubting of the postulate of regularity as in a questioning of the whole objectivistic position in value theory. We should observe, however, that it is logically permissible if not practically feasible to believe in the uniqueness of individual values in a sense that would allow their objectivity but deny their uniformity. I find such a view commonsensically implausible, but the many unsolved problems connected with the generalization of our singular value judgments may lead some hardy anarchists to defend it. I want in this final chapter to point out some of these problems and to indicate some of my ideas on them in the hope of stimulating interest in them and work on them.

Before embarking on this, however, I would like to set aside a possible, even if unlikely, misunderstanding. The sort of commonsensical, emotional intentionalism we have embraced does not countenance a direct appraisal of value-generalizations; it does not tell us to trust our feelings about the golden rule, the principle of an eye for an eye, or the canon that every work of art must be sincere or, again, must respect the materials used. I express this by saying that it is empirical. The basis of our knowledge of value is our feeling for individual acts or works of art. If any generalizations are justified they must be justified *as* generalizations upon such appraisals of single instances.

But this remark brings immediately to our attention the fact that we have no carefully developed and commonly accepted inductive logic for evaluative sentences (whether in the form of imperatives, normatives or value-predicative declaratives). It seems indubitable that such a logic, if it be true to our common modes of thought and expression, must be significantly different from the traditional inductive logic of descriptive declaratives.

In the first place, let us note, by one or two examples, that the behavior of quantifiers (if I may be allowed a technical expression) in an imperative or normative logic agreeable with everyday ways of talking cannot be the same as in the traditional logic of indicatives. From "Executioner, hang the condemned man" we must not derive "Someone, hang the condemned man," although we are allowed to infer "Someone will hang the condemned man" from "The executioner will hang him." Loss of specification (as indicated in going from a proper name or definite description to an "existential quantifier") may destroy legitimacy but leave truth intact. Another disanalogy appears in all-or-none evaluations. Suppose a company of soldiers to be in a desperate situation from which there is a chance that a bold move may extricate them. The commanding officer orders all to attack simultaneously. Has he ordered each to? Only on the further assumption that all the others obey. If, for example, an exploding shell kills all but one, the command is surely no longer binding upon that one. But with parallel indicatives it certainly follows without further qualifications that if all do attack each does. Consider a case of induction by simple enumeration. Imagine a boat capsized with the likelihood that no one uninvolved has seen her distress. The safest procedure for each of her crew is to lash himself to the overturned vessel, providing word of her plight gets ashore. The latter qualification demands that some one of her crew (every member of which is a valuable citizen and a good swimmer) undertake a dangerous swim. Now, from observing that each has secured himself to the boat we can properly conclude that all have, but from judging it good that this man has and that one also and so on for all the crew, we cannot conclude that it is good that all have made themselves fast.

These few instances must serve to show that generalized evaluative language conducts itself differently from its descriptive counterpart. It is a matter of regret that this area has not been adequately explored, but of gratification that interest in it seems to be growing. Now, if the very forms of our generalizations about values are disanalogous to those of our generalizations about fact, we may be confident that inductive procedures of justifying the former will present peculiar problems.

First, there is a question generated specifically by the type of analysis of evaluation given above. We saw that evaluation is a more complex form of intention than description. It embraces a suspended or frequently suspended assertion of fact. Are we to suppose, then, that there is a peculiar kind of uniformity made possible by this complexity, namely, a regularity in the relation between a (possible) fact and its worth? It may be harmless to admit this, but I see a danger in it. One is easily seduced, by this way of talking, into thinking that value, although peculiar, is just a sort of fact which can on occasion accompany others. Consider a type of hedonism. It does not define (intrinsic)

goodness as pleasantness; it asserts as a generalization that
everything pleasant is good. It is attractive to read this
as stating that every descriptive fact of something's being
pleasant is accompanied by a value-fact of that thing's
being good. But such a formulation is quite objectionable.
The goodness asserted, I would suppose, resides precisely
in the thing's being pleasant; it is not thought of as a property which, although actually present along with the pleasantness, could be there without it, exemplified in its own right.

If we resolutely resist this temptation it is permissible
on the approach we have taken to ask whether a single
type of fact, that is, the exemplification of some one
property, may not uniformly be related to value.   An
affirmative answer would commit us to a generalization
strikingly disanalogous to factual law. Take our hedonism
again.   Its assertion that everything pleasant is good can
perhaps be rendered, "It is good that everything be pleasant." This would parallel "It is a fact that everything is
pleasant." But whereas the latter is redundant (being reducible to "Everything is pleasant") the former is not.
Moreover, it is doubtful that "Everything is pleasant" has
the form of a law. If it is elliptical for "Everything which
I experience is pleasant," then it may be taken as a statement of factual uniformity, but hardly so as it stands.
Statements of factual uniformity have the design, "Everything exemplifying such-and-such a property also exemplifies such-and-such another" or "In so-and-so many cases
per hundred (or some other large number), exemplification of such-and-such a property is accompanied by exemplification of such-and-such another."   That is, factual
laws assert about how two or more properties go together.

It is attractive to think that if there be uniformities of
value they have a somewhat similar pattern, their assertion
being a claim about how two or more properties should go

together. This, of course, does seem frequently to be what we have in mind. When we say that keeping one's promises is always good or is in all cases one's duty we probably mean, more or less, that one's having made a promise, one's being in the circumstances of its fulfillment and one's carrying it out are appropriate, should go together, or whenever the first two obtain it is good that the third be true also. This case is thus quite analogous to saying that one always does keep one's promises, the difference being that it claims certain properties should go together rather than that they do.

It may be that besides this kind of value-uniformity there is another without parallel in the area of fact, namely, when the exemplification (actual or possible) of a single specified property is regularly accompanied by a certain value, say its goodness, quite independently of the other properties that may be present. I suppose, since I cannot rule this out logically, I should leave it an open question for empirical decision, but I confess that I feel uncomfortable about it. I don't think my trouble is procedural in a narrow sense. Suppose the candidate is pleasantness. We could then, by applying the coherence patterns mentioned in the last lecture, find it highly probable that this, that and the other thing's being pleasant is, in each instance and without any regularity in the other properties exemplified, excellent and as it should be. I believe my hesitation arises from a deeper source, namely from a conviction that what we in everyday life mean by our value-claims and approvals is the appropriateness of exemplification together of a plurality of properties. On this assumption, the kind of law we are now considering would conflict with the very nature of a value-claim. The widespread feeling that pleasantness in certain circumstances and connected with certain objects (for example, sadistic pleasure in another's suffering) is inappropriate and inherently wrong seems to bear me out. Pleasantness, then, would be good only when it is appropriate to other properties exemplified.

It must be admitted that the type of assumption just mentioned may be, and indeed has been, pushed to an extreme which destroys the possibility of any value-laws whatever. I refer to the supposition that every value-claim has the form, "It is appropriate that such-and-such a property be exemplified with just that unique totality of others present in the concrete case perceived or imagined." In a certain sense this supposition may be acceptable to empiricists, but not in any that makes value-uniformities impossible a priori. The sense I have in mind is simply that any singular claim of value is a claim that some property is appropriate to all the others exemplified by the individual in question; this allows us to analyze value-laws as generalizations upon these singular assertions, as saying that in every case in which such-and-such a property or properties is or are exemplified, some other is or would be appropriate in the total set. The appropriateness then would not be of an exemplification of only those few between which the uniformity holds, but of those in various concrete combinations with others, quite irrespective of the nature of the others. A value-law would then be comparable to a factual one. The gravitational law for freely falling bodies does not assert or imply anything about any body which has only temporal and spatial properties; it is about bodies endowed with whatever complex of further properties they may in each case be found concretely to possess.

But surely values are more concrete than facts and thus value-laws are more questionable than laws of fact? To the first, I would answer, "No"; to the second (omitting "thus"), "Yes." Facts are as unique and unrepetitive as are values; still, those who stress the singularity and incomparability of values have a point. This is especially true of artistic values (less so of moral). Critical canons in art may be harder to come by than physical laws of motion because of their greater complexity in the sense of their involving a greater number of independent variables. It must be remembered that even the laws of motion have their complexity, requiring what may be called "paper work," that is, symbolic computation. We do not directly perceive the constancy of the relations they assert. The properties that are perceived, however, are relatively few —space, time and (possibly) mass. With artistic canons, on the other hand, the number of irreducible perceptual properties appears to be very large. We may say that good art shows respect for the materials used, but surely this is a "blanket" way of speaking. Consider sculpture alone: our law covers the peculiarities of a vast range of substances (various woods and stones, iron, copper, plaster and so on), and it covers them in their directly perceived properties. So perhaps we can never hope to express the canon just mentioned in any general way that is less vague than the one adopted, greater precision arising only as we multiply it into subforms entangled in the actual procedures possible in handling specific materials. Something similar, though perhaps not so striking, may hold of moral rules and principles. I must leave this as a problem, but I hope not as one whose solution is ruled out a priori.

Another question I must table is that of the forms of inductive procedures that can be considered valid for establishing value-generalizations. Perhaps something analogous to Mill's methods may be found trustworthy. I should think, however, that the method of difference, if reliable at all, would be much less potent here than in its application in the area of fact. In the case of aesthetic value, for example, the appropriateness of some property may be destroyed by modifying one other, not because there is any generalizable relation to that one, but because the elimination of it breaks a total Gestalt. If you change the bright colors of Picasso's "Girl and Mirror" to somber hues you ruin the picture, but it doesn't follow that any picture is beautiful if painted in bright colors or that it is the bright colors alone that make this one a work of art. On the other hand, it may be that the method of agreement would play a much more important role than in factual generalization. Moreover, I have a feeling that simple enumeration would, in actual practice, turn out to be the best procedure available in most cases. But this is all virgin territory and calls for some venturesome empiricist to undertake its exploration.

Mill's methods apply to laws about individual occurrences. May there not be statistical or frequency laws in the area of value? Quite possibly; but I would think it implausible that all value-laws have this form. Consider what would be involved. We could say, in this type of formulation, that, on the average, telling the truth is good (or perhaps one's duty) in nine cases out of ten, but we could never, by the very nature of the uniformity asserted, specify which are the nine and which is the tenth, to put it crudely. That is, the law would have no implication for any individual instance of truth-telling, not even that its probability of being proper is nine-tenths. We might be able to live with moral rules of this kind, just as we have become accustomed to accident insurance based on actuarial findings (although in the latter case we justify our application of the "chances"—that is, the frequency distribution—to ourselves by supposing that there are laws determining individual accidents but that they are too complicated to be known). Nevertheless, I for one would feel very uncomfortable with the idea of legitimate moral codes that are inapplicable to individual acts and similarly uncomfortable, although less so, with the idea of critical canons that have no implications for individual works of art. I think there are two reasons for that discomfort. One is that in practice it gives one a sense of security in one's own appraisals of individual instances to find them in accord with general laws or, if one has no feeling for the given case, to deduce an evaluation of it from a general law. The other is that in theory it seems wrong to admit that appropriateness can be subject to completely chance variations; still, as empiricists we must admit this as a possibility.

Science has been successful not merely in finding empirical laws of fact but in constructing theories. These may be roughly characterized as premises, not themselves directly verifiable, from which a number of laws which are verifiable can be deduced. May we hope for something analogous for an empirical method of justifying value-generalizations? I think possibly we can and, indeed, that certain principles forming the bases of well-known ethical systems can be most fruitfully conceived as just such theories. Take the principle of utility. The attempt to establish it directly by induction would not get very far; that is, it does not appear to be a generalization of our moral feelings in individual cases. Most moral judgments of particular acts are not expressions of emotions directed toward the tendency of those acts to promote the general happiness. Our feeling in the individual case practically never embraces such a tendency. Now Mill, with his sense of reality, saw this and made the interesting suggestion that generally accepted moral rules be viewed as deducible from the principle of utility. However, this required some further premise, which he furnished by assuming that mankind's experience had functioned selectively to permit those rules to survive which on the whole did promote the general happiness. This assumption seems to me quite implausible (demanding an unconscious societal experience) and also unnecessary. What is needed is, on the one hand, an empirical method of establishing moral generalizations and, on the other, a deduction of those generalizations best established by such a method from the principle of utility. I have made suggestions relevant to the first requirement. The second can be satisfied only by considering individual moral laws in relation to the principle of utility. Many writers, with quite a different purpose, have suggested such deductions. It has been stated, for example, that telling the truth does, on the whole, facilitate social intercourse, business contracts, the acquisition of information and so on, and that these, in turn, are associated with more overall happiness than their opposites. If such subsidiary, factual generalizations can be verified with some reasonable degree of probability, then, I take it, the legitimacy of the rule requiring truth-telling can be deduced from the principle of utility. But if, now, we treat utility as a theory, then this deduction does not establish the rule; rather, the rule helps establish the theory, if (but only if) the rule is justified. That justification must be carried out completely independently of the theory of utility. We have seen how an emotive empiricism might do this.

I presume it is clear that I am not a utilitarian. Instead of the principle of utility I might have used that of self-realization as my example. The two could be set up as rival theories (in spite of what many have said, I think they do have somewhat different implications for moral behavior). But even if utility should prove the best theory for one using the method sketched above, such a one should not, I think, be called a "utilitarian," for he would be consistently and thoroughly empirical. His basis would not be a general principle justified either intuitively (as with Sidgwick) or as the only one men end with when their moral reasons are successively challenged (as with Bentham), but appraisals of individual acts.

And it is with this emphasis upon particular cases that I would like to close our inquiry. On the whole, the empiricists in value theory have been naturalists, reducing value judgments to factual statements of different varieties or treating them simply as themselves phenomena for factual study. On the other hand, non-naturalists have usually been intuitivists, a-priorists or authoritarians, not empiricists. The view I have outlined, by emphasizing the intentional character of emotions as revealed in everyday thought and speech, makes a genuinely empirical form of non-naturalism possible.

Index

Index